Last Trout
in Venice

The Far-Flung Escapades
of an Accidental Adventurer

Last Trout
in Venice

The Far-Flung Escapades
of an Accidental Adventurer

Doug Lansky

Travelers' Tales
San Francisco

Travelers' Tales and *Travelers' Tales Guides* are trademarks of Travelers' Tales, Inc., 330 Townsend Street, Suite 208, San Francisco, California 94107. www.travelerstales.com

Art Direction: Michele Wetherbee
Front Cover Design: Scott Idleman/Blink
Cover Photograph: Signe Lansky
Interior Design and Page Layout: Melanie Haage, using the fonts Bembo and Arbitrary Sans Serif

Distributed by Publishers Group West, 1700 Fourth Street, Berkeley, California 94710.

Library of Congress Cataloging-in-Publication Data
Lansky, Doug.
        Last trout in Venice / Doug Lansky.
             p.   cm.
        ISBN 1-885211-63-5 (alk. paper)
        1. Travel—Anecdotes. I. Title.

G151 .L366 2001
910–dc21   2001025005

First Edition
Printed in the United States
10 9 8 7 6 5 4 3 2 1

For my grandparents,
globetrotters at heart.

Table of Contents

Part Two
SLIGHTLY HIGHER EDUCATION

Part Three
RELATIVELY HARD CORE

Part Six
EASY DOES IT

Author's Plea to the Reader

Four-and-a-half Points to Maximize Your Reading Pleasure

(1) This book has less plot than a low-budget porn film. Come to think of it, nearly all travel writing does. (Life may frequently be stranger than fiction, but rarely does it have a better story line.) Therefore, I can see no reason to read this book in any particular order. I mean, I went to great lengths to put it in a particular order, but you'll probably enjoy it more if you just flip through and look for titles that catch your eye. Normally I'd suggest skipping the introduction, but it's the closest thing this book has to in-depth analysis, so you might want to check it out. The "Epilogue" isn't really an epilogue at all, but it is at the end of the book. It's one of the stories closest to my heart, so I hope you'll get to it at some point. In fact, there would be no harm in reading it first.

(2) Ideally you'll chuckle your way through the stories, eventually reaching the end of the book with the warm glow of having successfully traveled the world without a single case of amoebic dysentery. However, you may find the humor begins to lose its effect if you plug away at it for too long. At least, this is the case when I read humorous prose. So, for maximum effect, I'd suggest reading it in bite-size chunks. Friends have mentioned that the stories are just about the right length for a trip to the bathroom. You may wish to experiment with this, and should you decide to keep it near the throne, I'd be honored.

(3) For purposes of explanation, I sometimes need to pretend to know less about a subject than I actually do. For purposes of humor, I sometimes need to whine a bit, or make slightly insensitive remarks about dumb-ass foreigners and their moronic customs. Please take such comments with a grain of salt. No ill will is intended.

(4) You might not believe point number 3, so I'd like to bring in a totally neutral character witness: my wife, Signe:

> *Doug forgot to mention that if you combine the feigned lack of knowledge, occasional whining, and periodic insensitive remarks, his literary persona can, from time to time, come off as an Ugly American. In real life, I assure you, he is one of the most culturally aware travelers on the trail, and he does everything in his power to combat the negative American stereotype. He's so sensitive about this, if he does make a cultural blunder, I've seen him alter his accent and insist he's from another country, like Uzbeckistan. (He uses "-istan" countries frequently for this because he's convinced no one knows where they are. I'm not sure if Doug knows where they are.) On the other hand, he's not the most politically correct person walking the planet. If we pass by sewage in Venice, for example, he won't wax on about architecture or frescos or mesmerizing swirls of the oil layer drifting through the canals. He's not afraid to say the water "stinks" and that "he was sick for weeks after he inadvertently swallowed some when he fell into the canal." So there you go, Doug in a nutshell: a culturally aware, politically incorrect traveler who falls into canals and tells it as he swallows it.*

If these suggestions do not prove useful, you may try to salvage some enjoyment from the book this way:

(i) Buy a coffee table.

(ii) Place this book on it.

(iii) Glance at it wistfully from time to time.

(iv) Dust as needed.

Acknowledgments and Blame

It would be pretty pathetic if I waited until I got a book published to start thanking my wife for all she's done. It would be equally pathetic if I let the chance slip by to praise her again.

Thank you, my wife. I am ever so fortunate.

Moving right along to…my parents. They've done more for me than I can possibly relate, from wiping my nose to teaching me how to drive to telling me to drive slower and please turn down the radio while I'm at it. I couldn't wish for better parents. Love you, hug, etc.

I also must thank the publishers of this book, James and Larry. You'll be hard pressed to find two guys who work so hard, yet manage to spend so much time with their families. At least, that's what I assume they're doing when I can't get ahold of them. I've known them for six years now, and they're an absolute pleasure to work with, even on those rare occasions when I see them in person. Unlike most publishers today, James and Larry pour their sweat and blood into each book they publish. I'm thankful they decided to contribute their bodily fluids on this one.

I'd like to thank Lisa and Susan who checked this book for everything but quality prose. If you find any technical fault within these pages, this is who would prefer not to be blamed.

Finally, a heartfelt thanks to all the editors who reached deep down into their slush piles of unsolicited submissions and gave me a chance.

Introduction: Tourism 101

TOURISM IS AN ODD CONCEPT. AND I'M NOT JUST TALKING about eating vacuum-packed peanuts, buying fake Berlin Wall paperweights, and having exotic foreign encounters with concierges in well-kept hotels.

But are our travel habits any more odd than the tourist industry that is trying to attract us?

Just look at the slogans, which are basically a catchy way to say "Come and spend your money here." Ninety-nine percent of them sound so vague they could almost apply to any place on earth, yet are so overwhelmingly positive you have to wonder if the places actually exist.

Tourist boards spend millions of dollars on these campaigns (France alone has nearly a $70 million budget), but during my three days stomping around the International Tourism Exchange convention in Berlin asking about slogans, most of the tourist board representatives were hard pressed to tell me what their slogans were. They usually had to dig around for a brochure or consult with higher-ups to confirm. Then when I'd ask how important the slogans were, these people, who had only learned for themselves what they were thirty seconds ago, would look me right in the eye and say, "Oh, slogans make a huge difference."

One of the most popular slogan themes comes straight from the thoracic cavity. Samoa's is "Heart of the Pacific." Malawi prefers "The Warm Heart of Africa," and Latvia has "The Heartland of the Baltic." (The Latvians admit it's not that catchy, but they're working on a new one.) Guatemala's

Last Trout in Venice

"The Heart of the Mayan World" sounds the most precise, and Slovakia's "Forever in Your Heart" sounds like the title of some Rod Stewart song. Montenegro has "Great Heart of the Mediterranean"; Antigua and Barbuda have "The Heart of the Caribbean"; and Serbia has "Landscape Painted with Heart," which I can only assume bears no reference to the war.

Everyone wants to know a good secret, right? Well, Venezuela is "The Best Kept Secret in the Caribbean." However, they forgot to check with Madagascar, "The World's Best Kept Secret." Saint Kitts and Nevis used to use "Secret Caribbean," but I guess the secret thing wasn't fooling anyone, so they changed it to "Two Islands, One Paradise" (It sounds like a two-for-one deal).

It's no secret that many tourists prefer to make a beeline for stronger rays. It's not surprising, then, that the sun is also a preferred theme. Maldives has "On the Sunny Side of Life"; Slovenia has been using "Sunny Side of the Alps"; Spain had "Everything Under the Sun"; and Iran has the Jules Verne-sounding "A Passage to the Sun." Nigeria's "The Giant in the Sun" sounds like a bedtime story.

What separates each destination from its neighbors? Often it's not that much. Of course, they can't tell the tourists that. Everyone is anxious to distinguish their destination from the rest of the pack with something unique, something ...well, different. Santa Fe is "The City Different"; Estonia is "The Baltic Country with a Difference"; Oregon has the difficult-to-believe "Things Look Different Here"; and Kuwait says simply: "It's Different." Louisiana has "Come as You Are. Leave Different." (The women at the convention booth said this didn't translate very well into other languages.) And I'm pleased to see that peace has enabled Northern Ireland and the Republic of Ireland to start a joint tourism campaign. However, I can't say I'm overly thrilled with their slogan: "Live a Different Life." Are they suggesting you should go there and start cross-dressing?

Many destinations go for a dreamy, romantic slogan, and end up with something better suited for a prom theme. Pennsylvania has a classic: "Memories Last a Lifetime." Oman's would be favored by the decorating committee: "Beyond Your Imagination." New Jersey went for the mushy approach: "New Jersey and You...Perfect Together," while Iowa's sounds more appropriate for the junior prom: "You Make Me Smile." Tonga has set the stage for some heavy-handed chaperoning with "Land of Love," and Paraguay isn't far behind with "A Destination in Seduction."

Nearly every slogan could land in the vague category, but here are some of the vagueness winners. These are slogans that could, without exception, be used to describe every country, state, province, city, and town on the planet with only minimal exaggeration. Singapore has "So Easy to Enjoy"; Mauritius has "Fascination"; and Poland's "The Natural Choice" could even apply to a fruit drink or high-fiber breakfast cereal. Switzerland went for the very clever "Your Holiday," while neighbor Austria kicked in with "Holiday Breakaway." Turkey has "Welcome to Friends"; North Carolina has "A Better Place to Be" (better than what? The Ethiopian/Eritrean border?); and both Iceland and Thailand share the single word "Amazing" (Zimbabwe used to be "Amazing" as well, but recently changed). Fort Worth's was a little confusing: "Capturing the World's Attention." (Are they planning a terrorist strike soon?) Texas has "A Whole Other Country." (Apparently they've seceded from the Union without telling anyone.) Colombia's is "The Continent Country." I asked what that meant and they said, "It's like a whole continent in one country." Detroit abandoned "Expect a Lot" (I guess expectations got a bit too high) for "It's a Great Time."

Many of the tourist boards are now using more than one slogan to appeal to the various niche markets. This is what you might call a trend in the industry. Germany, for example, has "Culinary Germany" as one of these specialized slogans, though I doubt it impresses the French or Italians that much. "Fitness, Fun, and Beauty" is another. I gather it's supposed to appeal to the spa crowd, since these are not likely the first three words that come to mind when most people think of Germany. Still, the tourist board maintains an all-encompassing slogan: "Germany Wunderbar." I told the marketing manager I doubted all English speakers know that *wunderbar* means "wonderful." Some might misinterpret the slogan as some kind of Bavarian chocolate bar. But according to him (I won't reveal his name so he might keep his job), the "wunderbar" slogan was borrowed from "a Barbara Streisand song...or maybe a Nat King Cole song." He went to ask some higher-ups which was correct, then came back and told me it came from a Cole Porter song. Which song? No one knew.

Here are the world's worst slogans from my point of view. The hands-down winner is the city of Omaha, Nebraska, which came up with "OmAHA." (I think it's meant to be pronounced "Om Ahaaaa!" although I have to admit it still doesn't make me want to go there.) There are many runners-up, starting with Chile's "It's Going to Be In" (Does that mean Chile is currently out?). Pakistan insists you should "Visit Pakistan—Our Way." Sounds like you get a militant government escort. Quebec uses this slogan to attract Europeans: "America with a Certain *Je Ne Sais Quoi*." (I think "America with a Devalued Currency" would be more effective.) Washington state has "The Place You've Been Trying to Get To," which makes it sound like a fleet of motorists are driving around somewhere in Montana looking for it.

My favorites? I like Panama's "Much More Than a Canal" and Costa Rica's "No Artificial Ingredients" (their old one, "Tan Your Soul," is pretty good as well). I also liked the story behind Ethiopia's "Thirteen Months of Sunshine" —they do, in fact, have a different calendar. When the rest of the world switched over from the Julian to the Gregorian system in 1752 (almost 200 years after it was introduced by Pope Gregory XIII), Ethiopia decided not to get rid of their ten-day-long thirteenth month. So it's still 1994 there. They might try "Back to the Present" or just wait seven years and corner the market on the millennium celebration. Malta's slogan scores high marks across the board, managing to combine heart, sun, vagueness, and prom theme: "Where the Sun Shines from the Heart."

When I returned from Berlin, I had bags of travel brochures and travel magazines. I started flipping through them in the hope that I might discover what is actually luring tourists to all these destinations (since it can't possibly be the slogans).

What I saw were fine photographs of serene seas lightly lapping bleached beaches framed by palm trees jutting out over the water at preposterous angles that seemed like the horticultural equivalent of a dislocated shoulder. What each picture seemed to be saying was "This is Eden." That is, until you turn to the next page, which tells you "Or maybe

This is Eden." Then there's *Islands* magazine. It has so many pictures of tropical paradises, they've seemingly thrown in the towel and said, "We're not exactly sure what Eden is anymore, but if you get a subscription, we'll pummel you with new beaches every month."

Upon closer inspection of these paradise pictures, I noticed that there were no people in most of them. The beaches looked unstepped on, yet the skies were cloudless and the hotels were brand-spanking new. Why on Earth weren't there any tourists around? Were the hotels forced to close due to a fire code violation? Too many jellyfish in the water? Flip through brochures with this in mind and you'll think all these resorts are going out of business and the entire travel industry is in recession.

Of course the obvious rationale is that crowds of tourists obscure the "escape" image the tourist industry is trying to sell. In fact, with bodies shaped like eggplants, lesions that make Gorbachev's birthmark look like a freckle, and hair transplants that appear as if someone dropped divots and maneuvered them into place by foot, enough tourists can make any paradise downright unsightly. In short, to sell Eden, the tourist industry doesn't like to show tourism to potential tourists.

Which puts these competing Edens in an interesting bind. If there aren't supposed to be any tourists, what's going to happen when the people get there? (Especially as Eden gets more and more crowded, pushing the image further from reality and risking disillusioned visitors.) Imagine, for example, what the world would look like if the Russians, Indians, and Chinese started traveling as frequently as Americans. They'd outnumber us seven to one at every destination. At an already overcrowded site like Venice, you're looking at a jump from 25 million annual visitors to well over 100 million. It would sink in two years.

However, a few brochures seemed happy to show crowds. You'll rarely see an empty picture of the deck of a cruise ship. They don't want you to feel like you've been abandoned on the Lido deck. They want all passengers on board to feel they can "escape" together. (There's even a cruise ship called *Escape*—the idea being that you can somehow get away from it all while staying in more crowded conditions than you deal with on land.) The same photo policy applies to casinos, where they don't want you to feel like you're the only one losing money, and Disney World, although they're not likely to show people standing in intricately twisting lines or combing the parking lot in search of their cars.

Some photos display well-tanned professional models walking along an otherwise deserted beach, as if to say, "You could be this well-tanned, surgically enhanced, professional model walking along this deserted beach." But when *you* walk along this beach it will be lined with screaming kids and littered with snack wrappers because you can't afford to have the models' film crew block off the beach traffic and clean the area. We know this, but we fall in love with the image anyway.

A few travel companies are less concerned with the number of people in the photo—they are busy trying to convey "Educational" or "Eco" travel (for which brochure photographers faced the rather difficult task of making tourists look like they're learning, but having fun in the process). This is often typified by sitting on a tree-lodge balcony overlooking a rain forest or someone riding a camel in front of the Sphinx. Never mind that the main things the tourists in these photos actually learned were, in the first case, how to locate a beer in the rain forest and, in the second, how to bargain for thirty minutes, then pay $10 to get their picture taken on a camel.

The other thing I noticed about the images in these publications is what they *don't* show. It seems travelers want one thing before they go and another thing once they get there. They don't want to see, for example, pictures of film shops, kitsch souvenir stands, and McDonald's in the brochure, and they may even complain about this sort of capitalist invasion on the way in from the airport. But after a day or two in the country, this is where you'll find them, embracing creature comforts like a Greco-Roman wrestler. Fortunately, the tourist industry knows this. So they generally don't give tourists what they promised, they give tourists what tourists really want.

PART ONE

NEAR-MISS ADVENTURE

Penne Pinching

The World's Most Dangerous Car Rental

NAPLES, ITALY

I don't profess to know which city or country can lay claim to the world's worst drivers. It's certainly a close call. Portuguese drivers have one of the highest death rates. Egyptians prefer to drive with their horns instead of their headlights at night. The city of Athens doesn't appear ever to have passed any traffic laws. New Yorkers have not yet figured out why turn signals were installed on their cars. Residents of Los Angeles occasionally need semiautomatic weapons to gain access to their freeway system during rush hour. However, my informal survey of travelers revealed that Naples may take the prize as the worst. When I confronted several Neopolitans with this, they all said they are indeed the world's worst—and proud of it. "If you can drive in Naples," several Neopolitans boasted, "you can drive anywhere!"

So I went to Naples to rent a car.

If you stop and watch the traffic in Naples for a while, as I did when I walked out of the train station, you'll notice about 75 percent of the cars look like they've been ravaged by a cat with titanium claws. The source of the damage was not immediately apparent, since the cars on the road were not going much faster than the cars that were parked (in fact, it was often hard to tell which were double-parked and which were simply stuck in traffic).

For a little background information, I went to the tourist office. Here I met Franco Coda, who offered this driving advice for tourists: "Leave your car someplace and walk."

Next, I stopped by the Hertz office and asked the three men working behind the counter what advice they give to first-time drivers in Naples.

"Be careful at stoplights," one told me, "because most drivers don't respect them."

It seems red, yellow, and green lights are, in the eyes of Neopolitan drivers, just colors that should be obeyed no more than Christmas decorations.

Another Hertz employee warned me not to hang my arm out the window if I had any jewelry on it. Guys on scooters will drive up and snatch it. He also cautioned me to be wary when driving down one-way streets if I see a car coming toward me (the wrong way). He said I should wait and see how tough the guy looks before deciding if I want to back up.[1]

Giorgio Muro, the Hertz manager, concurred that all this was true and added that there are too many cars and not enough places to park. It takes most commuters ninety minutes to cross town (fifteen minutes without traffic) and another hour to find a parking spot. What Mr. Muro didn't

---

[1] The litmus test for how tough the person is is whether they point a gun at you while speaking.

understand was how everyone could afford to sit in their cars all day. "Are they unemployed or what?!"

Mr. Muro didn't have time to join me for a drive around town, so I walked ten yards over to the Avis office, where deputy manager Renato Vitaglione was given permission to come along for an hour if I paid for a full day's rental: $60. This included the usual insurance plan.

"What kind of deductible would I have to pay if the car got a little dent?" I asked.

"Around $300," said the manager. I swallowed hard, then asked how many one-day rentals come back with dents.

"At least 10 percent."

I swallowed hard again.

Renato, an all-around good sport who had an impressive grasp of English, joined me in my red Ford Fiesta. "Okay," he explained as I adjusted the rear-view mirror, "driving in Naples is like a video game. You just have to relax, stop thinking, and feel it in your stomach."

The only thing I could feel in my stomach was $300 worth of butterflies. I fastened my seat belt.

"What are you doing?!" Renato asked accusingly. I looked confused, so he explained. "No one in Naples wears seat belts. You want to look like a tourist?"

I unbuckled. Then Renato told me that about seven years ago, when a mandatory seat belt law was passed and briefly enforced, people started wearing t-shirts with a black stripe painted across the chest.

I had a death grip on the steering wheel as I pulled out from the curb and narrowly missed a collision with a speeding scooter that came out of nowhere. "They are mosquitoes," Renato said. "Just ignore them and they will buzz around you."

We came to the first traffic signal, but I couldn't tell what color the light was. "It's out of order," Renato said. "Just drive through." The next light was at a major intersection, and cars were stopping—but only if there was faster traffic coming from the other direction. In short, drivers approach intersections like New York pedestrians, with a cursory glance both ways during the approach. If there's not a car barreling down with intention to kill, it's O.K. to cross.

I asked why drivers ignored the traffic lights. "If they followed rules," he explained, "they'd be stuck in traffic for hours."

"But they are stuck in traffic for hours anyway," I pointed out.

"Well, yes," he admitted, "that's true."

"Why don't people use the bus or subway?" I asked.

"They do," Renato said. "That's the problem. It's crowded, hot, sweaty—no place you'd want to be stuck for hours if you owned a car."

My lesson also had an acoustic component. In Naples, the horn is not just a warning device, it's a musical instrument, and Renato played it beautifully. When we passed a voluptuous woman walking on the sidewalk, he reached over and hit the side of the horn, delivering three short, cute squeaks. No one looked over at us except the woman he was honking at, as if everyone knew that she was the object of the honk. Later, five machine-gun-style honks got the attention of a friend on the other side of the street. One quick blast warned a driver not to cut us off. When we were in a crowd of people, Renato reached over and honked with a short double-tap to the center of the horn, and people moved. A few were slow to get out of our way, and a two-second blast was required. This longer honk was quite effective, but protocol dictated that they shoot us nasty looks as they stepped aside.

Watching some Neopolitan drivers squeeze past me on the right, drive up on the curb, and triple-park, I wondered aloud how they'd ever passed their driver's tests. "They probably didn't," Renato answered. "Up until a few years ago, anyone could buy a black market license for around $600."

Now that I was getting the hang of it, it was time for a little sight-seeing. Renato gave me the three-second tour: "University there, church there, blonde there!" (Honk.)

Just then, I was motioned over to the side of the road by the police. What had I done wrong…I mean, besides running about twelve red lights, making umpteen illegal turns, and never using my blinker for any of them? As it turned out, this was a simple car insurance check. Renato had a nice chat with the police while they examined my driver's license and joked that it looked like a credit card. Or maybe they were just laughing at my picture.

As I pulled the car back up the Avis office, I asked Renato if it's tough to run a car rental business here. "Not really," he said. "Some people, mostly New Yorkers, love to come and drive here. To them, it's a sport."

Full Latex Jacket

Squeezing into Berlin's Infamous Kit Kat Club

BERLIN, GERMANY

I'M IN A BIT OF A BIND. NOT THE KIND THAT INVOLVES handcuffs and leather straps...at least, not yet. It's just that I'm faced with the rather daunting task of writing about my visit to Berlin's famous, erotic Kit Kat Club—while confining myself to tame, family-oriented words like "wild" and "group" and "fuckfest." I thought it would be interesting to find out for myself exactly what goes on there. And it was—starting with my first phone call to club owner Kristin, who told me I'd have to put on some kind of erotic costume if I wanted to get in.

This was more than a little intimidating because I'm an erotic fantasy novice, or beginner, or whatever the correct terminology is for someone who was completely ignorant about the details of kinky behavior—until Bill Clinton's impeachment trial.

When I arrived at the alternative clothing and fetish shop called Exciting, I introduced myself to the clerk, Jens, whose beard, leather vest, and beer gut gave him that middle-of-the-pack Hell's Angels look. He was wearing a baseball hat that said "Perv Police," and his English sounded like Schwarzenegger meets sex offender.

"I am eh stage und wideo pafoamer. Yoah noh vat I meen—S und M," Jens confided as he shook my hand. He gave me a quick tour of the tiny shop. I couldn't find anything that cost less than $100, except for a certain pair of shorts that I refused to even try on without modification. I held them up so Jens could see and said—I still can't believe I uttered these words—"Do you have these rubber shorts in my size, but without the, synthetic genitalia?"

"No," Jens said, unfazed. "But meebee jou cun buy dose leda schortz." He pointed to the shortest leather shorts I had ever seen, not to mention the only ones with metal spikes built into the crotch.

I ended up getting a one-piece outfit resembling the uniforms Olympic wrestlers wear, except it was black, made of latex, and about two sizes too small. The only thing more outrageous than putting it on was paying for it: $120. To distance myself from the wrestler motif, I also purchased a rubber spiked collar with silver glitter: $30(!!!). This would raise a few eyebrows—besides the ones that belong to the IRS auditor when he spots this $150 "research expense."

I couldn't leave the shop without finding out what some of the little gadgets were for. "What's that?" I pointed to a little metal device that might be used to tune a carburetor.

I can't tell you what it was, but the words "nipple" and "clamp" were involved. Jens then added—a little too proudly for my comfort level—"Jou cun even hang veights off it!"

At that moment, a featherweight twentysomething guy walked in. Jens greeted him warmly, then introduced us. "Dis iz Fabrizio, from Italy. Fabrizio iz eh bondage mastah."

We shook hands. Jens went on: "Ve vork togethah. Zome-
times he appeerz in my show."

"Oh, really?" I said, trying to sound impressed. "That's
great."

"Sometimes we make-a da spanking. You knowa da
spanking?" Fabrizio asked.

"Oh yes, I know da spanking," I assured them in an effort to quell the conversation, although I wasn't at all sure
we were speaking about the same thing.

I then pointed to a bottle on the top shelf behind the
counter. Jens took it down. "It iz forah anal sex und fist-
fahking." He undid the top and, before I had a chance to
pull back, rubbed some of the clear liquid on my hand.
"Zee," he boasted, "Dahrs no odah!" I didn't try to smell it.

"Go anda smell it," Fabrizio chimed in.

"I believe you," I said, but it was clear that this wasn't
good enough, so I smelled it. And I am happy to report that
it had no odor.

Standing there with anal sex and "fist-fahking" lubricant
on my hand, I tried to think of an intelligent question.[1]

Jens started going around the shop pointing things out
with language that would embarrass Dr. Ruth. There were
rings and clamps and handcuffs. Even a full-body rubber
suit. It costs about $500 and has double layers so you can
pump air between them.

"Pump it with air?" I asked in disbelief, a mental image
of the Sta-Puff Marshmallow Man beginning to form.

"Sensory deprivation," explained Fabrizio.

Jens took down another bottle. This one for "cleeening
out da asshohl afdah butt-fahking."

---

[1] "Can I oil my bicycle with it?" I finally asked.

To change the subject, I asked Jens what kind of customers he gets. "Noarmal peeple," he said, "like me und jou." Like me and you?!!

Almost on cue, a customer walked in—a hefty woman with multiple ear piercings. Another introduction. "She iz eh dominatrix," said Jens. We shook hands. What fantastic connections I was making!

Shopping complete, I went back to the hotel and got ready...for bed. (The club doesn't get going until 2 A.M.). At midnight, I donned the latex, then threw on some jeans and a sweater and made my way to the U-bahn.

I can tell you this from firsthand experience: latex doesn't breathe much. After only fifteen minutes I could feel sweat running down my legs and I began to wonder—purely from a dressing standpoint—if this is how it feels to be a superhero: wearing some constrictive, non-breathing, embarrassing costume underneath your regular clothing and trying not to fidget.

The entrance to the Kit Kat Club is a tiny staging area where you pay (about $15), strip down, and proceed through the next door into the actual club—a three-car-garage-size room with two toolshed-size rooms attached. The walls are decorated with comically pornographic glow-in-the-dark murals. Around the dance floor are two large swings and a freestanding wooden stockade.

The club was crowded, but not overly so. Maybe a hundred people. I can't describe the more outlandish outfits in the graphic detail they deserve without getting a bit ill, but about 15 percent of the crowd was displaying some sort of nudity. Another 40 percent (and I include myself in this group) had purchased overpriced outfits made of latex, rubber, and other materials not likely to decompose in the next millennium. Nonetheless, I felt most of the eyes turn toward me for inspection as I walked in. Did I look as ridiculous as I felt? I decided this was probably the case, and I proceeded to the nearest corner seat and tried to act as natural as possible under the circumstances.

After about twenty minutes, I made my way to the bar, pulled a 50 DM bill out of my sock and bought a Coke. I'm not sure what it cost, but I got plenty of change, mostly in coins, which, for lack of latex pockets, I had to deposit back into my sock. During the evening, most of the coins worked their way under my foot, which may have accounted for the coin-shaped blisters I discovered the next morning.

With a little courage, I slithered my way onto the dance floor. I'm going to sound like a musically out-of-it person when I say this, but I'm not a big fan of house, rave, or techno (I'm not even sure if there's a difference between these styles) and I've never been sure how you're supposed to dance to it. Plus, I wasn't particularly inspired by my latex jumpsuit and rubber spiked collar. Some people were clearly under the influence of mind-altering narcotics. Others—as is often the case—were mimicking the dance moves of those under the influence of mind-altering narcotics.

A few people were making out, but not more than you'd see at a senior prom. And no one was having sex on the dance floor, although this supposedly happens every so often. The biggest surprise was all the people who weren't wearing anything special: guys wearing jeans and t-shirts and women wearing clingy numbers you'd see in any other nightclub. Reportedly, many are tourists who come to peek—or, perhaps, peek to come. How had these people gotten in? I guess it's hard to know how much clothing they'll take off after they've been admitted. Obviously, the Kit Kat needs more Perv Police.

A Sticky Wicket

Getting a Grip on Cricket at Lord's

LONDON, ENGLAND

I WAS ACTUALLY WATCHING CRICKET FOR TWENTY minutes before I realized the game had started. Such is the level of excitement in this sport, which first struck me as a combination of baseball, golf, and waiting for a bus.

Lord's, the Wrigley Field of cricket, seemed like the ideal place to attempt to make some sense of this game, which first began in the 1800s and...well, I believe it's still being played. Subsequent games have been shortened to just five days, or perhaps five months—I'm not sure. My grasp of the game didn't get much better during my effort to unravel it.

Herefordshire (not a horse breed) was playing against Middlesex (not a compromising position) in a short one-day game when I showed up to watch. Apparently this was the sixtieth anniversary of the first televised cricket game. If that's not reason to celebrate, I don't know what is.

Keith, a fan I met in the bleachers who has been watching cricket for thirty years[1] tried to explain the game to me.

---

[1] Possibly the same game.

"It's like your baseball," he said. "The object is to get a lot of runs when you're batting and get the other team out when you're not."

"When you're not what?" I asked.

"Not in," he tried to clarify, "I mean, out."

Three sentences of explanation and I was confused already.

From what I gathered, the game works something like this: In an "innings"[2] there are sixty "overs" of six "legal balls."[3] The ball, a cross between a baseball and a shot put, is "bowled" at up to ninety miles per hour by a "bowler" who, before releasing it, is allowed to take a running start from as far away as Manchester.

The "wicket," a sometimes "sticky" stretch of grass the size of a long-jump pit that has been steamrolled before each "inning," is where the "batsman" tries to hit the ball while protecting three wooden croquet pegs called "stumps" and a wooden bar resting on top of them called a "bail." He does this with his ice-hockey goalie pads or his "bat," a flat paddle commonly used in America to butt-thump newly initiated fraternity pledges into their beer-drinking brotherhood.

If the "bowler" gets it past the "batsman" and knocks off the "bail," then the "bowler" gets hysterically happy and jumps around like a male cheerleader. If the "batsman" hits the ball, he tries to run back and forth across the "wicket" as many times as possible while carrying the "bat" and wearing his goalie pads. If a fielder manages to catch the ball

---

[2] Looks plural whether it is or not.

[3] They're legal as long as they're not "no balls" or "wide of the wicket" or "there's no foot in the crease," whatever that means.

before it hits the ground, he immediately throws it straight up in the air and jumps around like male cheerleader. That's about it. As Keith assured me, "It's really all quite simple."

It's hard to tell who the players are because they don't have numbers or names printed on their jerseys—they just wear white. And by "they," I mean both teams. If everyone stood on the field at once, it would look like a casting call for a bleach commercial. You can just barely distinguish the two umpires, who are dressed like cabana boys.

Spectators were forever coming and going, playing Scrabble, and reading books; they seemed to be watching cricket merely as a side distraction. Keith pointed out that it might go over well with an American audience because there's plenty of time for food and beverage consumption. In fact, while I was talking to Keith, they stopped the game so both the players and fans could take a forty-minute lunch break.

I decided to head up to the press box to get some expert opinions, but they were all having a beautifully catered lunch, so I helped myself to the buffet. Following lunch, I sat in the press viewing area, where I noticed that some of the cricket players had *returned to the field with their drinks,* which they just set next to themselves and continued to sip in between "overs," or perhaps "wickets."

There were about ten journalists in the room, including Norman, the vocal elder statesman of cricket; Derek, a former Cambridge cricket star who played on the British national team and now writes for a London newspaper; and Qamar, a Pakistani freelancer who has visited nearly every cricket ground in the world and will happily tell you about each of them.

"What just happened?" I asked Derek.

"He snicked it to the wicket keeper, who caught the edge."

"What?"

"Well," explained Norman, "you could also say he edged it to the wicket keeper, who caught the snick. It's really the same thing."

"Does the game have any exciting moments?" I asked the group, who all shot me a rather harsh glance.

"There's streaking," piped up Qamar. I asked him to explain. "At big international test matches," he went on, "there's often some attractive women who will streak across the field and try to hug the players."

"When does this happen?" I asked.

"Usually after the afternoon tea break," he said. And the others nodded their agreement.

I asked Stuart Weatherhead, the Lord's public relations director, if I could hit a few balls in the warm-up area. "Impossible. I can't allow it," he said, which simply made me want to do it even more. So I walked over to the batting cages, where two Middlesex players, David Nash and Tim Bloomfield, were warming up, and asked if I could hit a few. They told me it was no problem and loaned me some of their gear.

As I was strapping on the goalie leg pads, a man came over and told me I wasn't dressed in white. This is the sort of astute observation cricket officials are trained for.

"Really?" I said, looking at my navy blue slacks.

He said only the proper attire was allowed on the field, but that we could walk twenty yards and practice on the Astroturf, which we did.

And I have to tell you, cricket takes on an entirely new level of excitement when you're armed only with a fraternity paddle trying to fend off a ball that's coming at you at what seems like 400 miles per hour, and you're not wearing any private-part protection. Nash also threw some slower "spin balls" at me, which would skip off the ground about a yard in front of me, then kick up in any number of directions, except where I was swinging.

By the time I walked back to the press box, Stuart had already gotten word of my little practice session and was waiting for me with crossed arms.

"I thought I was perfectly clear that this was not allowed," he said. But we both knew that it was a bit late to do anything about it—and besides, it was tea time.

Quiz Show Bob

Behind the Scenes at The Price Is Right

HOLLYWOOD, CALIFORNIA

IT'S 4:00 A.M. ON A MONDAY MORNING AND I'M sitting outside CBS Studio City in the dark with *The Price is Right* audience. Think I'm nuts? Some of these people had been waiting since midnight. One man, who did not have any visible brain damage, spent $2,000 to fly his entire family down from Seattle just so they could see the show. There was even a small contingent from Armenia and a woman from Saudi Arabia. TV tourism is flourishing.

Over three hundred viewers get into the studio per show, and Signe and I had secured our spots in line. We were hoping to be one of the nine contestants picked to "Come on down" (not picked out of a hat, but hand-picked by the producer, Phillip. And everyone had a strategy to dazzle him).

Conventional wisdom was summed up best by Jenny, a young lady from Alabama: "You've got to be really, really perky." However, Jenny could out-perky Deborah Norville and it seemed futile to compete on that tack.

Some people brought gifts for Bob Barker and many had special t-shirts made up just for the occasion. Most read something like "Pick Me, Bob" or "I Love You, Bob" or "Bob, My Cat Is Neutered." One Brazilian man, who couldn't find his Berlitz guide that morning, had this shirt: "Nice People Wacth [*sic*] *The Price Is Right*."

I was sitting next to a thirty-one-year-old UPS delivery man named Michael Angelo. He was betting that he'd get picked on account of his unusual name. Plus, he had a broken wrist (sympathy points). Michael had come with some friends from Las Vegas, one of whom was a woman I will call Anne, which is not her real name, because Anne is a professional game-show player and, like a card-counter, would probably get barred from future shows if I revealed her identity.

Anne has won roughly $100,000 on game shows and has helped friends (by shouting from the audience) win another $50,000. For *Concentration,* she taped the shows, analyzed them, and determined that there were only nine patterns. She memorized them, then recorded the fastest time in the show's history when she was a contestant. She had studied *The Price Is Right* for nearly a year. She had memorized the prices for every product the show had given away in the past year and she knew what type of contestants the producers were looking for.

According to Anne, the producers picked people they believe their audience will support. First on her list are bubbly women with large tits and tight shorts. Second, if there's a big group in the audience, one member from that group will inevitably get picked. Military men and college athletes are also high odds provided they come in uniform. In essence, they want a diverse but large-breasted mix of middle America.

Why had Anne targeted this show? *The Price Is Right* is currently the easiest show in the country to get on—simply show up early and you've got a shot to be a contestant. I figure she could either be doing this or cracking codes for the Defense Department. She offered to help out Signe and me if either of us was selected.

At 7:30 A.M., we were given numbers marking our place in line and told to return at 9:30, where we waited in a different area that reminded me of a Greyhound bus station. Here, a CBS page came along, checked to see that we had photo ID and a social security number and then wrote our names on the famous oversized price-tag badges.

We sat around until noon, then were led in groups of ten past Phillip, the producer. Phillip seemed phony in a very authentic way that you only find in Hollywood. He asked us to say where we were from and what we did. It was clear that he wanted a short answer, not a conversation.

We were then led to a third waiting area, where we were not allowed to talk. After forty minutes of silence, we were led into the studio. Michael Angelo, a big fan of the show, couldn't believe how cheesy and small the studio was. The studio was in fact, extremely cheesy, with lots of lime green, hippie-orange, and Vegas-style blinking lights.

Rod Roddy, the rotund announcer, came out wearing a purple silk jacket over a screaming yellow silk shirt and whipped the crowd into a frenzy with several corny jokes. He even got us to recite the Audience Oath, for which we raised our right hands and promised to clap when we were told to clap, "oooh" and "aaah" when a new product was introduced and yell out "helpful" numbers when a contestant was trying to guess the price of something.

Then Bob Barker, the well-loved, well-tanned, and—according to several people sitting next to me who seemed up to date with this sort of thing—cosmetically altered host, came out and greeted us in his trademark suit, which may have reached its zenith of hipness among accountants in the seventies. He was also holding his trademark microphone, which looked like a beetle sitting on the end of a chopstick.

During the course of the show, nine people were called down. None of them were me. None were Signe, Michael Angelo, or Anne. Four of the contestants fell into the large-breasted category, though one of those was also a member of a big family-reunion group. There was a massive football player with a USC t-shirt and a few older contestants who looked like they had dressed to go fishing. They bid on such useful items as an amphibious vehicle and a "professional" popcorn cart. We all "ooohed" and "aaahed" as promised.

All the products were displayed by a team of models who acted so dippy they made Vanna White look like a feminist heroine.

The most exciting part of the show came when Bob said, "Rod, tell us what's behind curtain number two!" "How about this, Bob...a neeeew caaaaaaaar!" (Flashing lights, happy synthesizer music, applause.) A woman with breasts the size of bar stools nearly passed out and the stage hands had to come out and help her to her feet.

The second most exciting part occurred when, during a commercial break, someone dared to ask Bob how he keeps up his tan. Bob told us that he had had a few "spots" removed from his face recently but he got sidetracked and forgot to mention how he maintained his David Hasselhoff-like complexion.

The most interesting thing about the show, from my perspective, is that you have to pay tax—roughly 30 percent —on the merchandise you win. If you win an amphibious vehicle worth, say, $10,000, you have to come up with $3,000 if you want to keep it. Or, one could look at it this way: if you win something, you're winning the right to buy it at 70 percent off. Now, you have you ask yourself, would you run off and buy an amphibious vehicle, or a professional popcorn cart for that matter, if you knew you could get it at 70 percent off?

Neither would I.

Sick Man and the Sea

Fishing for Marlin off the Coast of Kenya

MALINDI, KENYA

I HAVE A GREAT IDEA FOR A NEW DIET PLAN—AND A catchy name to go with it. Allow me to introduce the Deep-Sea-Fishing-Off-Kenya's-Coast-During-Rainy-Season Weight Loss System. It's a bit spendy (a couple hundred bucks a day) but well worth it when you consider what you get: (1) Continuous Vomiting—you'll be retrieving food you haven't seen for days; (2) Abdominal Cramping—there's no faster way to tone up your abs; (3) Complete Appetite Suppression—between the rolling seas and watching the crew cut up fish heads on deck, the mere mention of food will send you to the edge of the boat. And that's not all! You get RESULTS! I lost five pounds in just seven hours at sea.

However, I can't take full responsibility for this amazing dietary discovery. I must give due credit to my inspiration: Ernest Hemingway, Nobel Prize winner and now weight-loss guru. The literary giant came to Malindi in search of big fish, and ended up landing a reputation for fishing these waters. Many of you may recall Hemingway's 1952 smash hit *The Old Man and the Sea,* which, unlike most classics, was actually read because—as you no doubt remember—it was the only required text even shorter than the Cliff's Notes version. Today, as a tribute, there's a hotel called Hemingway's that specializes in deep-sea fishing, although Ernest does not share in the profits from this venture because, among other reasons, he's dead.

Using Hemingway's name for promotion is no unique phenomenon in the tourist industry. Bars around the world have made their fortunes based solely on the fact that Mr. E. Hemingway once passed out in their cloakroom. Having cut a wide swath across the globe (picking up the odd drink or two along the way), he can take personal credit for an entire genre of tourism. I even remember seeing a restaurant in Madrid that boasted "Hemingway never ate here!"

It's tough to coordinate a long trip with the best season for every activity you wish to undertake. And it seems I had missed the ideal time to experience the waters off Kenya's coast from a fishing and boating standpoint. I had arrived during the rainy-and-rough-seas season. On the upside, it was also low tourist season, which allowed me to charter my own boat for a full day for only $175. The normal rates for this are closer to $500.

I negotiated the deal on the street with a man named Nelson (I got the feeling that every deal in Malindi goes through Nelson), who put me in touch with Captain Youseff, who was in charge of the nearly modern fishing boat, *Lady Nana.*

All the fishing equipment on *Lady Nana* looked up to snuff when I boarded, but I could see the boat lacked any navigational equipment and, more importantly, power. It was propelled by two 40-horsepower engines that only ran at half-thrust. If you're not familiar with horsepower, that's like powering a cruise ship with a class of second graders kicking at the back.

This sort of power is fine for trolling along, but I began to worry as we headed out into seas with swells the height of residential telephone poles. On the surface of these massive swells were three-foot-high waves, and on these waves was nine-inch-high chop. It was often hard to tell if we were even moving forward. Which probably didn't matter much because Captain Youseff was usually spinning us in circles. If someone could figure out a way to re-create this motion for just a minute, they'd make a fortune at amusement parks from teenagers in search of the ultimate nauseating experience.

Two of the faster boats that had passed us on the way out to sea made quick retreats, which Youseff credited to seasick clients. The day before, Youseff himself had to turn back after just ninety minutes with two Italian fishermen who were puking from the moment the boat left the dock.

Needless to say, I spent the first several hours with my head over the railing. Signe, whom I now call Iron Stomach, didn't so much as spit.

Meanwhile, the three crew members were frantically attaching lures, letting out the six separate fishing lines, pulling them in, uncrossing them, and adjusting the friction on the various reels.

It couldn't have been more than five minutes before we got a hit on one of the lines. The crew flew into action. I was directed into the fisherman's chair—a bolted seat in the center of the deck with a groin-level holder for the rod. I pulled back, then reeled in the slack as I lowered the tip of the rod forward. I had seen this technique used on a TV infomercial. It was just a matter of minutes before I had my head back over the railing while Iron Stomach reeled in the fish.

It was a silvery, torpedo-like bonito, sixteen, maybe eighteen inches long. About four pounds. This was pretty exciting stuff for us. Iron Stomach started snapping photos while I held up the catch and posed with the crew. I thought they were smiling at first, but I soon realized it was a look of confusion. I soon found out why. They extricated the fish from the line, attached some hooks to it, and threw it back in. Apparently we had just caught the bait.

We reeled in a few more bonitos over the next hour. Or parts of them. We had a hard time reeling them in quick enough. Most of this was the fault of my stomach. While reeling in the fish, I'd get sick, hand the rod to Iron Stomach, and run to the edge of the boat to cough up a few organs.

Meanwhile, marlin—we were always told it was a marlin—would swim along and take a bite out of our bonitos before we could land them. For some time, it seemed as if we were just pulling in a series of bonito heads.

I did manage to hold myself together long enough to pull in the day's big catch: a fairly unimpressive twenty-pound kingfish. Landing him took about ten minutes of reeling, and if I wasn't soaked by the cold rain the entire time, I might have even broken a sweat.

After seven hours, $175, and five pounds of Hemingway Miracle Weight Loss, we had about five bonito heads, a few whole bonitos, and a kingfish to show for it. As we disembarked, leaving the fish for the crew, I suggested Youseff think about renaming his boat.

"To what?" he asked.

"Hemingway Never Puked Here."

Storming Morocco

Meeting and Greeting in Arabic Africa

FEZ, MOROCCO

MOST PEOPLE WHO POP OVER TO MOROCCO ON THE forty-five-minute ferry ride from Spain figure, it's summer, it's Africa....it must be really hot. They input this into the tourist data bank on the top floor and come up with: "I'll wear a tank top, some shorts, and an expensive pair of sandals." To Moroccan hustlers—a generally harmless but over-anxious and relentless sales force who call themselves "guides" or "students" and comprise roughly 99 percent of the ferry's welcoming committee—this is like taping $100 bills all over your body and sitting down for coffee at the White House.

There's no avoiding this welcoming committee. Moroccans have been trying to "guide" tourists into their uncles' carpet shops since the Precambrian era, when the only tourists who came ashore still had gills. Today, after centuries of horror stories, many tourists are so nervous they wouldn't recognize a genuine Moroccan if they stepped on one while fleeing from the hustlers. And to be

honest, it's hard to tell. They all promise they are not hustlers. This, in fact, is Rule Number One: *Anyone who tells
you right away that they're not a hustler is a hustler.*

When I arrived in Tangier, it took nearly forever to get
off the ferry. Everyone was being funneled down a tiny
boarding ramp. It was like filing Macy's Thanksgiving Day
Parade through my sister's closet.

When I finally disembarked, I was waved through customs and into a waiting area packed with fifty Moroccan
men with official badges who were nagging just like the
hustlers. I decided to keep my head down and march past
them as quickly as possible. A few men kept pace alongside
me, nonetheless.

"Hey, why are you walking so fast?" asked one.

"Be friendly. I am international—like Coca-Cola,"
added another.

"Don't be paranoid," contributed a third.

"I am not a guide," said the first one, "I am a student. I
just want to practice English. Look." He pulled out a photo
album of his "European girlfriends," which he conveniently
happened to have with him, and started telling me the names
of each one and which countries they came from. They
looked like professional models, and upon second glance I
noticed they were. Was this supposed to impress me—a guy
who walks around with a collection of professional-model
wallet photos and claims they were one-night stands?

When he saw I wasn't buying it (whatever I was supposed to be buying), he said, "O.K., better to have 1 mosquito than 100 mosquitoes. I can keep the others away."
Now he was speaking my language.

However, I knew where I was going—to the train station 200 meters in front of me. I told him I didn't require

his services and wished him luck. He continued to follow me. To my dismay, a traveler near me stepped in and told the man to "*imshee*," (piss off)—sadly enough, the first Arabic word most tourists learn. It's insulting and rarely produces any results. I didn't really mind this guy following me. At least he had put away his photo album.

When I reached the train station, Mr. Wallet Photo demanded money for guiding me there. This was normal. The technique of leading from behind was mastered in Morocco and has since been adopted by most Western leaders. I gave him a French coin and moved on while he examined it.

I boarded my train for Fez and entered a compartment with three Moroccan men. No one said a word. After twenty minutes I initiated conversation. The man next to me, it turned out, had been living in Boston for eight years and was returning to visit his family and buy more crafts for his import business. Another was born and lived in France. And the last, from a small town in the mountains, had never actually met a foreigner before. They were afraid to start talking to me because of Rule Number One.

Before long, the Frenchman borrowed my guitar and did a wicked impersonation of—I know you may find this hard to believe—Johnny Cash. The rest of us sang along, or hummed, or forced a smile all the way to Fez.

In Fez I noticed that some of the tourists, tired of standing out in their Western attire and urged on by hustlers to try to fit in, had purchased a djellabah and were already walking around in the traditional Arabic loose-fitting robes. Now they didn't look like tourists just off the boat, they looked even more gullible. The hustlers could spot these people from the other side of the Atlas Mountains, and now they had something to chat about. "Excuse me, sir," I over-heard in the market, "I see you have discovered our traditional dress. It's very becoming on you. It is very comfortable, is it not? My father owns a shop with some of the most beautiful djellabahs in the world. You come. I take you there. I am actually a guide...and a student."

I asked one young Moroccan for directions to a hotel in Fez. He said he was walking that way if I wanted to join him, so I did. Adil was a twenty-three-year-old college student majoring in English. He seemed nervous while we were walking. I asked him if there was anything wrong. He uneasily asked if I would mind stopping by the police station with him so I could register as his official friend. "That way," he explained, "I won't get into trouble for guiding you to your hotel."

I was more anxious to get to my hotel than I was to wait around a Moroccan police station, so I had him point me in the right direction and we met for dinner at his house. Adil lived with his parents, brothers, and sister in a one-bedroom apartment in the slum area of Fez. The bathroom, with a Bunsen burner on the floor, also served as the kitchen and Adil and his two siblings, now grown up, still slept on the floor in the living room, which was also the dining room and the there's-just-static-on-TV-but-let's-watch-it-anyway room.

I spent the following three days with Adil's family, communicating through Adil and more hand gestures than you're legally allowed to use in the game of Pictionary. The food was fantastic and the hospitality heartwarming. It was hard to leave.

I especially dreaded the onslaught of "guiding" offers at the train station. But as much as I disliked maneuvering through the raucous greeters, I had to admit, it does give Morocco a certain charm. And you can't hold anything against the Moroccans for their hustlers. We have them in the U.S., too. Only we know them by another name: tele-marketers.

Driving Fjords

Riding a Cargo Ship up the Coast of Patagonia

PUERTO MONTT, CHILE

THE CARGO SHIP WAS FOUR HOURS LATE, WHICH FOR the Navimag shipping company was slightly ahead of schedule. I was waiting in the port with about 150 back-packers and 150 Chileans to board the *Puerto Eden*, a cross between an oil tanker and a tug boat, for a four-day ride north, up the coast of Patagonia—Chile's answer to a cruise of the Norwegian fjords.

Getting on the boat was the first trick. It's known to depart as much as a day late and sometimes several hours early, which always leaves several unhappy travelers standing on the dock clutching their tickets like losing bets at the racetrack.

When the boat began loading at 9:30 on Thursday evening, there was a mild stampede to get on board, especially for us economy-class (also known as dungeon-class or burro-class) ticket holders. We didn't want to end up with one of the infamous top bunks of the triple-decker beds, which can be ascended easily, but only with proper climbing equipment. These beds have about three inches of head room so those with large noses have to wedge themselves in to sleep. I managed a middle bed, which was just fine. No sheets were furnished, but there was a blanket with a noticeable urine smell, a pillow with a slight vomit smell, and a reading light.

There were two twenty-four-occupant dungeon-class barracks, each equipped with two toilets and one shower. (If you work out the bathroom math and factor in the typical peak usage times, that translates roughly to a waiting period of just long enough to pee on your blanket and vomit on your pillow.) These barracks were located at the very bottom of the ship, near, I think, the engine room, the generator, the anchor-chain-dropping-room, and the rock-concert-amplifier-testing room. That is to say, it was deafening.

The boat left port early Friday morning without fanfare while most passengers were sleeping. We were awakened by the first of many announcements at 9:00 A.M., alerting us that something vaguely resembling breakfast was now being served.

That day the captain called a meeting for first-class passengers in the lounge, which also served as the main dining room, the video room, the non-duty-free shopping room, the à la carte cafeteria, the smoking room, the non-smoking room, the bingo parlor, the bar, and the discotheque. I crept in unnoticed while the captain and first mate made eloquent speeches about the voyage, explained safety procedures, and answered questions—in Spanish. The captain then asked, in Spanish, if anybody needed to have anything explained in English. Naturally, the forty or so passengers who couldn't understand Spanish didn't speak up at this point. And this information was never conveyed to those who couldn't understand Spanish or to the people without first-class accommodations, leaving most of the passengers clueless in the event of an emergency.

That doesn't mean the crew couldn't communicate with us. When there was a whale sighting, announcements were also made in English, French, and Portuguese. But this didn't work out so well. By the time the whale sighting was translated into several languages and people straggled out to the decks, the whales were long gone.

What did we do all day? Not much. It felt like an airport waiting room. People read, watched *The Empire Strikes Back* for the twelfth time, played cards, drank, and slept. The scenery was indeed "breathtakingly beautiful and rugged," as the brochure had promised, but it was too windy and cold to stay outside for long, so we usually settled for glancing out the ship's small windows.

On Saturday we arrived in Puerto Eden, the ship's namesake, and were awakened by the release of the anchor. In dungeon class it sounded as if the anchor had been dropped through the hull. We weren't sure whether to wake up or abandon ship.

Nearly 200 of us decided to go ashore in the small transport vessels, which required wearing, by law, an enormous orange life preserver. Once on shore they were so cumbersome that the easiest way to carry them was simply to keep wearing them. So we were easily identifiable to the locals—and probably to any passing spacecraft as well.

After a few hours waddling around town buying prerequisite souvenirs, we went back to the ship and prepared ourselves for the open-sea crossing. Right on schedule,[1] the

---

[1] One hour late.

boat started rocking with the fifteen-foot swells. And, right on time, half of us started puking our guts out.

The waves, relative to the boat's size, were not threatening, but they hit the boat directly on her port side and created an astoundingly nauseating effect. Many of my fellow travelers took Dramamine and wandered down to their bunks to pass out. Others drank wine or beer until they passed out. Either way, we were aiming for the same goal. In the middle of the most turbulent part of the voyage, the captain sarcastically read a poem over the PA system. I didn't catch all of it, but I managed to pick up these lines: "There are people around the world suffering more than you. Suffer well. There is still hope."

The highlight of the trip came on the third day, when we had a tug-of-war with the crew on the nearly empty upper cargo deck. It was the crew versus the gringos, and we travelers, who had spent too much time sitting on buses and not enough time loading and unloading cargo ships, got trounced. Or, rather, dragged.

Team Gringo fared better in the ensuing soccer match. Roberto from Milan, Sven from Brussels, and Stephan from Germany dominated our otherwise outgunned attack. Adding to the excitement was the cargo deck's metal rivets, holding buckles, and twenty-ton freight elevator. A simple pass could ricochet in any direction—as could your patella if you didn't watch out. Playing soccer there was like water skiing in the Persian Gulf during Operation Desert Storm.

We had an award ceremony after the game. Not for the players, but for all passengers. Everyone received a certificate of achievement for, I suppose, shelling out $150 or more to spend four days on a cargo ship. After the last award was given, a crew member attached a disco ball to the ceiling and we tried to dance to some Patagonian folk songs. Two people had birthdays, which occasioned a song and more drinking. Several passengers went out on deck to see the stars; others could see stars in the comfort of their own heads.

Next thing most of us recall was waking at 6 A.M. by the sound of the anchor dropping through our skulls. We had arrived at our destination in Puerto Montt. We gathered our things and went ashore, where many of us became instantly landsick—the strange sensation of "feeling" the land sway and wanting to puke on any stationary object.

We suffered well.

PART TWO

SLIGHTLY HIGHER
EDUCATION

Last Trout in Venice

A Gondola Lesson on the Grand Canal

 VENICE, ITALY

I'M SITTING HERE IN MY WET UNDERWEAR ON THE SIDE of the Grand Canal waiting for my clothes to dry. I have a burning blister on my thumb, algae stains coating my pants, and I just swallowed a mouthful of Venetian canal water, which I believe is melting the lining of my stomach. To top things off, I'm pretty sure some passing tourist caught my accidental plunge into the canal on tape and will soon be making thousands of dollars on *Italy's Funniest Home Videos* at my expense.

How I ended up in the Grand Canal should come as no surprise. I was taking gondola-driving lessons. Hardly a "must-do" in Venice. Most simply come for the romance: cozy strolls along the canals with the sound of distant bells, small waves gently lapping against ancient palazzos, and, of course, the enchanting footsteps of the 25 million tourists with white sneakers who annually trample this slowly sinking city of 75,000 residents.

Learning to drive a gondola on the Grand Canal is like

learning to ride a bike on the Long Island Expressway. Whizzing up and down the canals are water buses, water taxis, private cruising boats, supply boats taking food and merchandise to the stores, plus all the other gondolas—over 400 of them. There are no driving lanes on this busy aquatic road. You can drive on the left side or the right or straight down the middle if you please. The only rule I saw observed is that the biggest boat has the right of way. Does this method work? Well, during my three days in Venice, there were three separate boating fatalities.

The way I figured, there's only one oar, they move slowly, what could be easier? As I learned from Lucca, a fortysomething gondolier I met who offered to show me the ropes, it would be much easier to learn to pilot an oil tanker through the Strait of Magellan.

There aren't any gondola-driving schools, as such. Most gondoliers learn their trade from their fathers or uncles and then inherit the boats from them. Lucca's father, however, was a Venetian glassblower, and Lucca was a dental hygienist. Eight years ago, he decided he wanted to spend less time fighting plaque and more time at peace with the outdoors, so he put down $20,000, bought a gondola, and taught himself how to drive it.

The world is quite familiar with the famous image of these thirty-seven-foot black canoes. What many may not know is how they actually move. The *remo*, or oar, rests in a wooden fork that protrudes from the rear right of the gondola. Unlike in a row boat, you don't lift the paddle out of the water to bring it back into position for the next stroke. Nor do you push off the bottom off the canal, as I once suspected. Instead, you push forward, then feather the *remo* back under the water. And unlike in a canoe, you can't start paddling on the other side to compensate for a turn. Everything has to be done from the fork.

After a short demonstration, Lucca held onto a pole on the side of the canal to keep the boat in place while I gave it a try. My first problem was that the oar kept popping out of the fork, and the waves, the tidal current, and the substantial weight of the *remo* made it hard to get it back in position. After I managed a few strokes, he let go and we were off.

Immediately, Lucca began issuing a seemingly impossible set of instructions. The first was "Use your legs," then "Get your whole body into the rowing motion." As I did this, the oar popped out of the fork and I struggled to put it back in, nearly falling overboard in the process. With no forward momentum, we began drifting out of control toward several boats. "Look forward," he said, oblivious to the fact that I couldn't get the *remo* back into the fork while looking forward, and simply looking forward wouldn't accomplish much except indicate which side of the gondola to jump from before we were rammed by a much larger boat.

Signe, who had come along for the ride, looked almost as nervous as I did, and I could see her plotting how to abandon ship without getting the camera wet.

Fortunately the other boat drivers had guessed that an absolute moron was piloting this gondola, and they managed to get out of our way. It probably helped that Lucca was standing at the front of the boat, making the "get the hell out of the way" signal.

Next Lucca wanted me to turn the boat around. He took the *remo* and demonstrated. It looked simple, and, surprisingly, it was. However, this technique only applied to turning the boat to the left. Turning it to the right was near impossible. The only way I could make a 90-degree right turn was to turn the boat to the left 270 degrees.

About forty minutes into the lesson, my arms felt as if I had been doing forty minutes of push-ups. I didn't have enough strength left to shake hands. So Lucca took over, did some more demonstrations, and guided the boat back to the gondola station for a break. Back on land, Lucca taught me the time-honored tradition of how gondoliers discreetly urinate into the canal: you stand on the dock, hold a board in one hand, and lean it against a pole to form a little...well, teepee, and do your business under that.

I asked Lucca about the singing. After all, all gondoliers sing, don't they? "I don't sing," he said.

"But I thought you all had to at least do 'O Sole Mio.'"

"No," he said, "that's a myth. There are a handful of gondoliers who sing, but you almost always have to pay extra for a singer to come along."

"Customers pay $100 for forty-five minutes in a gondola and don't get a singer included?" I asked, incredulous.

"No, that costs extra. Didn't I just tell you that?"

When I began to get some feeling back in my arms, we pushed out for the next lesson. With considerably more traffic and bigger waves, it looked twice as intimidating. After a few near spills, my oar slipped out of the fork and I finally lost complete balance and tumbled rather dramatically (twirling arms and all) into the drink, which, unfortunately, is what I inadvertently did as I came up for air. The water was murky brown, more biologically aggressive than anything in Iraq's arsenal, and tasted like month-old dishwater mixed with ammonia and a touch of diesel oil. I tried (unsuccessfully) to forget that Lucca and I had peed into this canal less than an hour ago.

Lucca couldn't stop laughing. Neither could Signe, who managed to capture the entire event on film. So did a water taxi full of video-taping tourists.

Just then something brushed my leg. I tried not to think what it could be, but my mind was already racing. A lone trout that had innocently mistaken the water for cappuccino? The dead body of a tourist weighted down by camera equipment?

I swam hurriedly to the edge of the canal and pulled myself up onto the algae-covered wooden steps. Lucca managed to control his hysterics just enough to broadcast my spill to every passing gondola driver. "Into the water," he yelled to anyone willing to listen, "like *Baywatch* Pamela Anderson."

Signe bought some beers for Lucca and the other gondola drivers at the station, where Lucca, the human instant replay, began a series of dry-run reenactments of my fall, which he continued for thirty minutes while I dried off, much to the enjoyment of the other gondoliers and a newlywed couple standing nearby.

"In a hundred years," he joked, "come back and we'll be singing about the American who fell into the canal."

"You will?" I asked, falling right into his trap.

"No, the singers will. And you'll have to pay extra to hear it."

Sumo Cum Laude

Learning to Live Large in the Sumo Ring

TOKYO, JAPAN

I ALWAYS THOUGHT THAT SUMO WRESTLING WAS PRETTY straightforward: two pachyderm-sized, coronary bypass candidates grab hold of their opponents' G-strings and try to toss each other out of a clay ring onto a diminutive business executive sitting in the front row who has—quite reasonably, I think—paid thousands of dollars for this privilege.

This was my philistine grasp of the sport prior to my visit to Tokyo University's Sumo Club. Until then, my entire experience with sumo was comprised of occasionally watching sumo highlights on *EuroSport* (Europe's answer to ESPN) late at night with a couple of friends. We all genuinely enjoyed these sumo clips...on an impressively superficial level.

The *EuroSport* commentators had no idea what they were talking about, and before they could even finish mispronouncing the wrestlers' names, the fifteen-second matches were over. Our appreciation revolved mostly around gawking at the sheer bulk of these corpulent athletes and wondering how they figured into Darwin's theory of evolution. Every so often, one of us would chime in with a nugget of insightful commentary, such as "Get a load of that guy—must have swallowed Marlon Brando and the bean bag chair he was sitting on."

When I arrived in Japan, I didn't want to miss the opportunity to gain a deeper appreciation of this sport. By going behind the scenes, maybe even trying sumo myself, I thought I might make some sense out of it. Tokyo University's Sumo Club, where up-and-coming sumo wrestlers live and eat, seemed like the perfect place to go, especially since it was the only club that granted me access.

After watching the fifteen or so wrestlers perform a series of thundering leg stomps, butt slaps, and squats around the *dohyo,* a kiddy-pool-sized, clay-surfaced ring in the club's coffee-shop-sized gym, it was my turn to get suited up. One of the junior wrestlers had me disrobe while he prepared the *mawashi.* You'd never know it to look at someone wearing one of these off-white G-strings, but they're thirty feet long and as wide as a sweat towel. He folded the material to the width of a fire hose—which is exactly what the material felt like—and began the human-origami task of wrapping me up in it.

I lost track of how many times the *mawashi* was looped around my waist because I was busy thinking that I had never seen a man up close who was in more dire need of a bra. When he was done, there was still about a yard and a half of *mawashi* left over, which seemed to puzzle him. Clearly, these things were not designed for people with less than an eighty-inch waist. By comparison, my six-foot-tall, 185-pound frame looked as skeletal as Ally McBeal. He cut off the excess, stepped back, and I caught a glimpse of myself in the mirror. It looked like I was heading off to a photo shoot for the World's Most Incredible Wedgie.

I swallowed hard, then walked out into the training area. Every head turned. I couldn't have felt more naked than if I actually were.

After failing to achieve the basic sumo-squatting posture—legs spread wide, knees bent ninety degrees, toes pointed out, hips forward—without falling over or suffering back spasms, we moved on to the famous lift-one-leg-up-slap-yourself-on-the-ass-then-put-your-leg-back-down warm-up routine. I liked this exercise much better because I could at least manage a decent slap. The rest of the maneuver, however, required more balance and strength than I could muster.

I did several instructed scampers across the ring—incorrectly, I'm sure—before it was time for some body ramming. For this, I was supposed to lean forward, brace myself, and let this 270-pound behemoth launch me out of the *dohyo*. Surprisingly, it didn't hurt all that much...compared to, say, getting rammed by a Lincoln Navigator.

Then it was my turn to do the ramming. Naturally, I was pretty ineffective. I'm not even sure if he felt the impact. His layers of cellulite, I discovered, were covering a brick wall of muscle. And I was also a bit hesitant because the proper way to ram involves jamming your hands under the arms of the ram-ee. This guy's armpits were positively cavernous; I think I was able to insert my arms right up to my elbows. I was also concerned I might—in ramming haste—inadvertently deliver a blow to a sensitive spot and he might get upset and sit on me.

After he determined I had taken enough abuse, it was

time for me to wrestle the chief of the club. Sumo seems to be a one-weight-class-fits-all sport, though the winners often have a size advantage. The chief was not the heaviest man in the room (which is not to say he looked like a pushover). I was giving him these "ha, ha, go easy on me" looks; he was growling like a hungry pit bull, pacing the ring, and staring me down. I began to worry.

We tossed some salt into the *dohyo*, performing a traditional purification ritual. How salt can purify anything but popcorn, I don't know. And neither, apparently, do these wrestlers. Every time I asked (via translator) why they did certain rituals, they just shrugged. It's not part of Japanese nature to ask, they said.

The chief and I placed our fists in *shikiri* position—on the two opposing lines in the center of the ring. Sweat dripped from his brow. Come to think of it, sweat was dripping from all the wrestlers' brows all the time. It seemed their tremendous girth made standing and breathing an aerobic sport.

Fortunately, we skipped the ramming and moved straight to the grapple. It felt as if his feet were rooted into the clay. I couldn't move him. He went pretty easy on me, allowing me to struggle for nearly thirty seconds before he grabbed my *mawashi* and hauled me off the ground. I had not been given a wedgie since the third grade, and my entire body froze, Frankenstein-style, as he did this, allowing him to casually fling me out of the *dohyo*.

My abridged lesson was over, and it left me with a new-found appreciation for the wrestlers' athleticism, a slightly better understanding of the sport, and a bruised rib or two. But my biggest sumo challenge was still ahead...joining them for dinner.

I sat next to the chief on a floor cushion as these om-nivores began to feed. In the center of this floor feast was a cauldron of *chankonabe* stew, the caloric staple of the sumo diet. The pace of the meal was frantic—no time wasted on conversation—and I reached my about-to-explode limit well before these guys stopped shoveling down their meals. But when the wrestlers stood up to leave, I noticed they had left a good deal of food behind. The chief explained why with a laugh as he patted his paunch. They were just taking a breather; this had only been the first course.

A Kick in the Head

Thai Kickboxing School Enrollment

BANGKOK, THAILAND

I SUPPOSE YOU COULD SAY I'M A TRAINED THAI KICK-boxer. However, at my current level of training, I'd have a hard time kicking the Queen Mother in the shins...without his security detail. Even Stephen Hawking could probably beat the crap out of me. But then how much can you expect after just one week of kickboxing school?

Muay Thai (directly translated as Thai boxing, and more loosely as kickboxing) has been Thailand's national sport for hundreds of years. The combatants not only kick, they trip, push, and elbow—although *elbowboxing* doesn't have quite the same ring to it. Kickboxing may have a barbaric image, but compared to its past, it is now quite sportsmanlike. Before 1920, the fighters didn't wear boxing gloves, just horsehide hand-wraps dipped in glue and covered with small shards of glass and shell. Not surprisingly, fights occasionally ended with a trip to the morgue.

This blood sport was not what I had in mind when I enrolled at Jitti's Gym. The sign out front said that Jitti specializes in training foreigners. In fact, he's trained five European champions and five Japanese champions. And he does all right with the locals as well: eleven champions of Thailand, including Jitti himself. Many of the world's top kickboxers pass through here at some point, though you wouldn't realize it to look at the open-air gym. It was located down an alley, half in a driveway, half under a shelter, with two punching bags and one battered ring. The place smells of tiger balm and mosquito spray and the walls are covered with weathered snapshots of kickboxers.

I didn't recognize Jitti when I first met him. I asked his name and he just pointed to his shirt, which said "Jitti's Gym," and handed me a jump rope.

After forty-five minutes of jumping rope barefoot in the cement alley, my arms were limp and the skin was peeling off my feet at an alarming rate. I waited for Jitti to tell me when to stop. It seemed he never would. In fact, he never did. Another trainer finally called me over to get my hands wrapped.

With my hands taped and sweat covering my body, I felt an awful lot like a kickboxer, but for the minor detail that I had no idea what I was doing.

"Go into the ring and shadowbox," Jitti said.

My body went rigid with fear. Shadowbox? In the ring? There were a handful of kickboxers in the gym. I'd sooner play air guitar in front of Eric Clapton.

I slid between the ragged ropes of the ring, stepping onto a mat that looked and felt like a drained waterbed mattress. It was dull metallic, patched together with duct tape, and covered with dried spit. I had no idea how to even begin shadowboxing. A Swede was warming up near the ring, so I leaned over and asked for some advice.

"Just do it like you see in the movies." Apparently, I had just asked for boxing tips from a graduate of the Ingmar Bergman school of combat.

With little choice, I followed his advice and did some tentative shuckin' and jivin', punching at the air with neither the force nor technique to so much as bruise a March of Dimes poster child. After five or ten minutes, my style hadn't improved but I was starting to get into it, bouncing around the ring delivering semiformidable blows to my imaginary opponent. Suddenly I glanced up to see that about fifteen hardcore kickboxers had entered the gym and were staring at me. If they all weren't supported by visibly sculpted abdominal muscles, they probably would have fallen to the ground and collectively wet themselves.[1]

After what seemed an eternity of embarrassment, Jitti sent me to "work the bag." This meant punching a hanging

---

[1] One of these hardcore guys turned out to be a bit of a head case. Before I left on my last day, I interviewed Jitti and explained for the first time that I was planning to write a story about my boxing experience. This Italian guy, the number two rated lightweight in Italy, who hadn't said boo to me during the week, saw me interviewing Jitti and stopped sparring just long enough to ask if he could meet me in an hour for a drink. I agreed. At the bar, he asked me what I learned about Jitti during my interview. I asked why he wanted to know. "Is for an Italian kickboxing magazine," he told me. It crossed my mind to tell him to go interview Jitti himself, but I was feeling pretty relaxed after the long workout, especially now that I had a beer in my hand. I glanced at my notes.

"He was the Thai lightweight champion ten years ago," I said.

He began to write the sentence out long hand. "More slowly," he said, "when was he champion?"

"Teeeennnn yeeeaaarrrrs aaagooo."

continued

body bag that felt like Rush Limbaugh was hiding inside. I was also supposed to elbow it. Knee it. Inflict every kind of punishment possible on a bag. I thought I'd start out with a kick, as this was kickboxing. So I gave it a really good whack with the top of my foot and—I say this knowing that I may sound like a total weenie here—it really hurt. I mean I thought I might have busted my foot. I was absolutely writhing in pain. And there wasn't much to do but suck it up and keep working the bag. I worked it, now with considerably less enthusiasm, until I was pretty sure the bag had given me an all-around good pummeling.

Then Jitti called me into the ring again. He was suited up with pads this time. I was fitted with boxing gloves. Jitti would say "jab" or "kick" or "elbow" and I was supposed to do all these things to his pads. I don't know how long our little round lasted, but I was so sore after it ended, I barely had enough strength to hobble down the street a hundred

---

"He was lightweight?"

"Yes."

And so it went for about forty-five minutes, which seemed pretty long considering my interview with Jitti lasted no more than fifteen minutes.

"What Jitti's fight record?" he asked me.

"I don't know," I shrugged.

"You don't know?!"

"No."

"Why you no ask him?"

"Because I didn't feel it was vital for my story."

"Why not?!" he demanded.

"I don't know, I just didn't ask him."

"I can't believe you no ask him."

continued

yards to my hostel on Koh San Road, where I slept for about thirteen hours.

The next day offered more or less the same thing, except I was paired with a different trainer in the ring—this one younger and considerably more aggressive than Jitti. If I let either arm down for a millisecond, he'd punch or kick me in the head. If I held my arms too high, I got a punch in the gut. The blows were not meant to hurt me much, just teach me a lesson. After fifteen minutes and about twenty "instructional" whacks to the head and stomach, I couldn't move. I slowly regained some strength and limped down the road to my hostel, although this time I was tempted to take a taxi.

Over the next several days I evolved into a walking bottle of Vicks VapoRub. The Thai version of this product is Tiger Balm, which I'd rub on my legs with it before and after each practice and a few other times during the day to

---

"Look," I explained, "you can ask him yourself. He speaks English. You don't need to limit your writing to my notes."

"Oh, I don't do writing."

"You don't?"

"No, I send notes to editor friend at magazine. He writes article."

"You're kidding."

"No, is truth."

"And he puts your name on the article?"

"Yes."

"Just for providing the notes?"

"Yes."

"So will I get my name on the article as well?"

"Why should you get name on article?"

"Never mind."

keep my muscles from cramping. All my clothes smelled like Tiger Balm. My bed smelled like Tiger Balm. Even my hostel room toilet seat smelled like Tiger Balm. When I walked down the street, heads would turn...usually in the other direction.

On the fourth day, I bought some Thai boxing shorts. I felt a little uneasy wearing them to practice, as if I were about to commit the boxing equivalent of showing up on the bunny slope with a $1,000 ski outfit—even though the shorts cost me only $7. The shorts also had something written across the crotch in big Thai letters. The fact that I couldn't read it made me more than a little nervous. In all likelihood, the words meant something like "Fierce Warrior" or "Thai Boxer." But, for all I know, I could have purchased a pair from the Tourist-Idiot Series emblazoned with "Wuss" or "Tiny Penis" or—God forbid—"Kick Me Here."

By the end of the week, I felt I had made some improvement with my fighting technique. Unfortunately, my body was so sore after three hours of daily practice, I had a hard time lifting my legs off the ground. So my kickboxing would only be effective against an opponent two-and-a-half feet tall. Or, to put it another way, I'd just about have a fighting chance against a garden gnome.

Beating the Water with an Expensive Stick

Fly-Fishing 101 in the Rocky Mountains

COLORADO SPRINGS, COLORADO

It was a fascinating sight: men standing around in rubber pants, adjusting their flies, whipping their rods back and forth, and occasionally exclaiming, "Look here. I've got a big one!"

Of course, I'm talking about fly-fishing. And here in the shadow of Pike's Peak, fly-fishing isn't just a hobby, it's a way of life.

I, too, was wearing rubber pants, also known as "water-proof support hose," as I stood in the parking lot of Deckers, a well-fished stream just twenty minutes north of Pikes Peak, waiting for my 9 A.M. beginners' fly-fishing class to start.

I spent a good deal of time checking my gear, or just fidgeting with it. I carried my rented $300 rod and reel awkwardly, like a new father trying to find a comfortable position to hold his baby. I spent ten minutes studying my sunglasses, trying to determine whether or not they were polarized because I had been told it was a crucial feature. And I rechecked the new fishing license I had picked up at 7-Eleven for $5 to make sure it had the right date and to see if there was a coupon on the back for a Big Gulp.

Fellow classmates Carol and Libby, both in their forties, arrived together. Mark, also around forty, and the only one who confessed any experience, came on his own.

Our barrel-chested, bearded instructor was also named Mark. Instructor Mark was leading the class with Antonio, a junior high-school teacher and part-time fishing guide. Both of these men were wearing vests covered with several hundred dollars worth of fly-fishing gizmos, though to the untrained eye it just looked like they were wearing colorful wads of lint.

Instructor Mark announced that we would start fishing with nymphs. This didn't do much in the way of explanation because neither Libby, Carol, nor myself would have been able to pick a nymph out of a police lineup, even if everyone but the nymph was wearing a police uniform. Quite simply, Instructor Mark explained, a nymph stays underwater, not on top of it, and nymphs should *definitely* not be confused with streamers, emergers, wet flies, or dry flies.

To determine exactly what sort of nymph we needed, Instructor Mark took a ping-pong net, or something that looked like a ping-pong net but probably cost ten times as much, and used it as a strainer to collect some debris floating in the river. He pulled up a couple of squirmy critters the size of head lice and studied them with more interest than you'd expect a grown man to display when looking at aquatic larvae. This, he explained (as if it weren't evident), was part of the fun of fly-fishing.

Antonio baited his line with one of these creatures and immediately caught a trout to show us how it's done. More impressive than the catch was how gentle he was with the fish once he'd caught it. He wet his hands before touching it so he wouldn't damage its scales, and extracted the fly like a thoracic surgeon. Then he held the trout in the water and stroked it while it regained its strength. All of this would have been quite touching if Antonio hadn't just jerked the fish to shore by its mouth with a hook.

The whole process seemed a bit like lassoing a bird flying south for the winter and yanking it to the ground, then fluffing up its feathers and letting it go. It just didn't look like that much fun for the trout, some of which, Instructor Mark explained, had been caught more than of *forty times.*

I must have caught one of these professional trout. The moment I got him on the line, he swam straight to shore and beached himself. He knew the drill. He didn't even blink when we took a flash photo of me holding him. Possibly because he didn't have eyelids.

I caught two trout and hooked myself three times (twice on my shirt and once on my hat). Libby and Carol each caught two trout, plus each other. And even Signe, who put down her camera for twenty minutes, caught two fish and Libby's shirt. Mark the student was having bad luck, probably because he jinxed himself by telling everyone he had experience.

I have to admit, it felt good to pull in a fish, to see the line jerk and the trout jump out of the water. I felt a bit like Brad Pitt in the movie *A River Runs through It*.[1] But when I had to reach down to get the hook out of the trout, it didn't quite seem worth the fish's discomfort. Especially when he wriggled out of my hands and fell on a rock. I can certainly

---

[1] Except, of course, that I'm a little taller.

understand the appeal of fishing, though. Particularly when extremely expensive speedboats are involved.

The fish we caught were called rainbow trout and brown trout. The rainbows were imported from California and the browns were brought in from Germany. I began to wonder what I was doing in Colorado, aside from sponging off my old college roommate, Tim, for a few days.

Tim, an experienced fly-fisherman, had witnessed my casting and told me, with that honesty one reserves for good friends, I was "whacking water with a stick." To learn to appreciate another aspect of the sport, I let Tim try to teach me to tie a fly.

This was confusing right from the start. The size of the lines and hooks get smaller as the numbers that describe them get bigger. Each fly-tying tool has a complex name, and the only thing more complex than the name of the tool is the name of the fly you're trying to tie with it. At least, when in doubt, you can call any lure a "fly"—even lures that stay underwater, look like worms, and have less chance of achieving flight than a hypoglycemic hippopotamus.

"Here," Tim would say. "This is the little doohickie. And this is the big doohickie. You just hold this chicken feather and wrap this 22-pound line around—Doug, keep watching—and make this loop. Then you just—Doug, see how easy this is?—tuck this thingy under here while letting the little number 14 doohickie hang. You see that, right?" And I would tell Tim, "Yes, I saw it." Then he'd hand me the tools and I'd just sit there, thinking I would have a better chance of constructing a Boeing 747.[2]

---

[2] So that's what I did. I just made a life-size Boeing 747 right there with Tim's fly-fishing tools.

After one hour, Tim had talked me through making a "ten-minute" fly. It looked very artistic…in a Picasso sort of way. There appeared to be two heads, two abdomens, and several stray appendages. Tim and Signe just stared at it, not quite sure what to say. Perhaps, I suggested, it might perform well in the streams near Chernobyl.

Tuning Out

A Crash Course in Swiss Yodeling

 AROSA, SWITZERLAND

I HAVE A GOOD DEAL OF EXPERIENCE WITH MUSIC, stemming from my eighth-grade music appreciation class, which I had to attend after getting kicked out of choir. ("Well," I was told rather frankly by the choirmaster, "I don't think you're quite eighth-grade-choir material.") Music appreciation was filled with the bulk of the hockey team and the guys from woodshop class. The object, as far as I could tell, was to try to appreciate music that no eighth grader would ever willingly listen to. We were only interested in appreciating popular music of the day, such as a song called "Abracadabra."[1]

So, with my rich history of music and singing, I set off to the Swiss Alps ski resort of Arosa with the hope that my voice might be better suited for the vocal gymnastics of yodeling. I joined up with a yodeling clinic, but I made it quite clear to everyone, just in case my voice didn't hold

---

[1] Actual lyrics: "Abra, abra, cadabra. I'm gonna reach out and grab ya!"

up, that I was a writer, not a singer. "Hi, I'm Doug, and I don't sing" is exactly what I said.

On Monday morning, about thirty yodeling pupils were divided into two groups that would switch throughout the day between instructors Mrs. Bea Salzmann and Mrs. Vreni Rubi, two of Switzerland's top yodelers (the country has 25,000 of them).

My first class was with Mrs. Salzmann, who had that well-groomed flight-attendant look—I half expected her to start pointing out the emergency exits and restrooms. However, the first order of the day was breathing exercises. Most of these felt rather silly to a nonsinger such as myself. For instance, we'd meander around the room, and when we'd bump into someone, we'd put our finger to our lips and give them a librarian's "shhhhhh." After that we were told to jump up and down while making those SWAT-team noises ("hut-hut-hut-hut-hut-hut"). We kept this up for about an hour. Don't ask me what it has to do with yodeling, but apparently, it's vital.

In the next class, Mrs. Rubi was wearing a leotard, causing me to wonder what sort of yodeling exercises we were in for now. (Step aerobics?) It turned out there was very little jumping around at all. In fact, we even did a little singing, and it became immediately evident that nearly all of these people were professional singers or yodelers already.

When it was my turn to sing "Scales," I picked up my pen and notepad and claimed that under normal circumstances (such as in my car with the radio on full blast and the windows up) I would love to sing, but unfortunately at this moment I'm simply too busy writing. The group wouldn't let me get away with this; after enough razzing, I rattled off all the disclaimers I could think of and gave it a try.

I'm pretty sure I didn't hit a single note correctly, because I happen to know for a fact that I'm completely tone deaf. If you played a simple note, I probably couldn't tell you what it was with nine guesses. In addition to not hitting the correct notes, Mrs. Rubi informed me I was singing with the wrong part of my body. I always thought you sang with your mouth. WRONG! Just ask any singer, and they'll back me up on this. As it turns out, you sing with your diaphragm, an internal muscle most people can't distinguish from a carburetor, whose only function I knew of was the junior-high party belch.[2]

In order to loosen up my diaphragm, Mrs. Rubi had me stand with my back flat against the wall and my knees bent. Facing me, she would sing a few notes and I was supposed to sing them back to her in a loud, forceful way. She sang "Do, Re, Me." I sang it back, sort of. We continued this until I reached the high end of my range, which didn't take long.

When my voice cracked as if the God of Puberty himself had touched my vocal chords, Mrs. Rubi put both her hands on the center of my chest and started pumping aggressively, as if she were trying to administer CPR. Startled, I stopped singing, but she urged me to continue. The result was stunning. My crackling voice became full (one might even say pleasant sounding) and I was able to go several notes higher.[3]

My fellow yodelmates cheered me on and I pumped my fists in the air when I hit the top of the scale. I felt ready to run off over the mountains with Julie Andrews.

---

[2] Apparently, you also sing with your nasal pharynx and your sinuses, but how this is possible, I have no idea.

[3] But don't ask me which notes they were.

Back in Mrs. Salzmann's class, we finally heard some yodeling demonstrations. Swiss yodeling is much different from its Austrian cousin. The Swiss style is much slower, more melodic, and has more of a cow-calling folk tune to it. The Austrians, the Swiss say, are more concerned with the speed of their yodeling than making it sound nice. And to my untrained ears, I'd have to say that there is some truth to this.

In the last class of the day, Mrs. Rubi had us make the yodel sound, which involves changing from a "throaty" voice to a falsetto and back, so that your Adam's apple bobs playfully. However, when I did it, no matter how hard I tried, I sounded like I was imitating a donkey's "hee-haw."

Mrs. Rubi separated the men and women and had us yodel in two groups. There were only two other men, one a semiprofessional opera singer from Germany who also dabbled in Gregorian chant, and the other an elderly Swiss yodeler with decades of experience. The German held the sheet of music while the Swiss guy and I looked on from either side.

When they began singing, it didn't take long for me to realize that (1) I hadn't the faintest idea how to read music; (2) I couldn't pronounce the Swiss-German lyrics; and (3) I couldn't stay in tune with the rest of the group. Actually, I didn't notice point number 3, but everyone else did, and with just a few laser-like glances they were able to convey this message.

When class ended, I tried to assess my progress. I still couldn't read music; I could only hold a tune while getting CPR; and I never managed to yodel per se. But I did attract the attention of a few mules in the area.

Bake Sale

Enrolling in the Cordon Bleu

PARIS, FRANCE

WHEN READER LARRY MCPEWITT WROTE ME "WHEN are you going to start *researching* your stories?!" I decided it was time to do something about it. So, after securing a place in a pastry-making course at the world-famous Cordon Bleu cooking school, I scoured the finest bakeries in France, painstakingly stuffing myself with triple-layer chocolate pies, raspberry tarts, crème éclairs, caramel nut rolls, and enough fudge-meringue to trigger adult-onset diabetes from just looking at them. I researched pastries until my blood-sugar level looked like Donald Trump's income-tax figures.

Of course what you're probably wondering is how I ever got accepted to the Cordon Bleu, the Harvard of cooking schools, the alma mater of Julia Child, a school with over one hundred years of culinary history. Did I send them a photo of my PB and J with the crusts cut off or my burnt macaroni and cheese à la Kraft? Did I write an essay on the properties of finger Jello or fifty uses for Cheese

Whiz? Actually, there is no application procedure for their one-day workshops other than signing up and sending them $150 for five hours of instruction, lunch included.

The Cordon Bleu, located in southwestern Paris, looked like your typical unimaginative 1970s cement, six-story, Parisian apartment building, except it said Cordon Bleu on the outside. It also said Cordon Bleu on the inside. Everywhere I looked there was a sign that told me I was at The Cordon Bleu. I was issued a white apron that said Cordon Bleu and given a little Cordon Bleu towel to tuck into my Cordon Bleu apron. Like everyone else, I was even made to wear a little white Cordon Bleu beanie hat. At least, everyone else's hat said Cordon Bleu. Mine just had the number 56 printed on it, which made me look remarkably like a potato peeler in the Navy.

My class of twelve was, it turned out, almost entirely American. There were blonde twin sisters from Texas, an elderly woman from California who'd written a book about French watermills (though I never got up the courage to ask her what a French watermill was), two women from Utah, one named Suzanne who kept telling everyone (I lost track after the fifth time I heard her say it) that Utah was the site of the 2002 winter Olympics, a French-born American who had a restaurant and catering service in North Carolina, and a few other American tourists who were sick of the Louvre.

There was also a quiet, young couple from Mexico City and an elderly French woman—the only person in the room who didn't understand English and, as a result, was paradoxically left out of most conversation.

The big news was that a photographer from *Bon Appetit Magazine* was there to photograph our class. He spent the first thirty minutes moaning about the horrible lighting, then remedied the situation by bringing in enough wattage to illuminate the landing strip at Charles de Gaulle Airport. I was, apparently, the only one in the room who had never heard of this magazine, and was thus not terribly excited by the prospects of getting photographed for it. A few others were discreetly clawing their way into each picture frame.

The classroom was about double the size of a health-club Jacuzzi with one trampoline-sized counter in the center and ovens, freezers, and sinks on the perimeter. Nothing looked ornate, just well used and practical. While the *Bon Appetit* photographer was darting around with his light meter and camera, Masterchef Duchene began demonstrating and the translator began translating, sometimes with painful accuracy.

Masterchef Duchene: "*Cracquez...*

Translator: "Crack...."

Masterschef Duchene: "*les oeufs...*"

Translator: "the eggs..."

Masterchef Duchene: "*et mettez...*"

Translator: "and put..."

Masterchef Duchene: "*les ouefs...*"

Translator: "the eggs...."

Masterchef Duchene: "*dans le bol.*"

ALL OF US: "in the bowl!"

The translation was generally fine but probably unnecessary, since Masterchef Duchene spoke fluent English. But his French was about the only reminder that we were still in France.

Masterchef Duchene was thirty-something, very friendly, down to earth, and on the skinny side. He was also a Meilleur Ouverer de France, which translates directly as

"Better Opener of France," and, according to his two American assistants, this translates more loosely as "Will Never Have To Worry About Finding A Job."

Masterchef Duchene started using his hands to mix some butter and flour while explaining the molecular properties of what was occurring in the bowl. He even drew us a diagram of what we were trying to achieve with our molecules. ("You want the molecules to look like this.") And he was always talking about gluten. I had no idea what gluten was, but Masterchef Duchene didn't seem like the person to ask. It would have been like going to a Wimbledon press conference and asking Pete Sampras what a backhand was.

We watched Masterchef Duchene make an Alsacian filling while we took notes with our doughy fingers. Then he demonstrated how to fill the pie shell and line the top with apricots, with the two assistants standing behind him and handing him instruments like surgical nurses. "Apricots?" I heard the Texas twins whisper, "Yuck."

"It is very important," Masterchef Duchene told us, "that the apricots have been baked and marinated."

"Does that mean apricots out of a can?" I asked.

"*Oui.*"

Everyone gasped. The twins put their hands over their mouths. The restaurateur looked white. Canned fruit at the Cordon Bleu?! We had stumbled upon some culinary dirty laundry. It was as if we had learned there was rat poison in Coke's secret formula. (Little Disclaimer: There's no rat poison in Coke, as far as I know.)

We made four pies in all: apricot, pear, apple, and plum. Masterchef Duchene made all the fillings and the assistants prepared the fruit with can openers while we took notes.

Then we filled our pies and gave them to the assistants to bake. Much to my delight and engorgement, finger dipping—sticking your finger in the bowl of filling, then licking it—was actually encouraged.

[Pause for *Bon Appetit* photo: Light meter check. Fix hair. Hold up pies. Smile. Everyone move closer together. Little more. Keep smiling. Act natural. Flash.]

I left at the end of the day with three cavities, tight pants, and a diploma that stated in French something to the effect of: "[insert name here] was able to produce four pies with the help of two professional Cordon Bleu assistants who prepared the ingredients, washed the pots, and scraped the baking sheets. Congratulations!"

Riding the Rolex

Taking a Whack at Polo School

THE COTSWALDS, ENGLAND

UNTIL RECENTLY, THE CLOSEST I GOT TO THE GAME OF polo was getting sprayed with Ralph Lauren's cologne by an overzealous attendant as I walked through an airport duty-free shop. I couldn't tell you how many players there are on a team, how many points you get for a goal, or even if cross-checking is allowed.

All I knew for certain was that polo players have names like Sir Rumpus Pompous VI, are required to compare Rolexes for a least three minutes between games, and send their polo ponies to Swiss health spas for grooming.

To get a taste of the famous sport people know so little about, I took a train to the Cotswolds, an hour west of London, and enrolled at John P. Smails's Edgeworth Polo School. The tall, mustachioed, ever-so-kind Mr. Smails, who plays polo with Prince Charles and prefers to be called John P., started me out on a wooden horse in the polo equivalent of a batting cage.

The polo mallet is like a long croquet mallet with a carbon fiber or cane shaft. However, you don't hit the ball (a solid chunk of plastic) with the rounded ends, as you do in croquet; you use the side, which makes things only slightly easier. There are six basic strokes: off-side forehand, on-side backhand, under-the-tail, under-the-neck, over-the-Rolex, and into-the-Jaguar. After nearly an hour of swinging the mallet, it was time to move on to an actual horse.

First, John P. thought I should get some background information. He had me watch a forty-five-minute video about the sport. I learned that polo traces its roots to Prussia, where they've found evidence of the game in cave paintings.[1] It migrated to the horse-savvy Mongolians, then into China. From there it made its way to India, where the British army picked it up and brought it home. Polo then spread to Argentina, where equestrian-orientated Argentines learned it so well that they now dominate the sport worldwide. And to the U.S., where everyday, run-of-the-mill Americans such as Ralph Lauren use it to promote exclusive retail products.

It's worth noting that polo ponies aren't actually ponies; they're horses. They were called ponies because smaller horses were preferred for reaching the ground with the mallet. Many top ponies are actually racehorses that didn't quite make it on the track. Owners like John P. buy them and, with three years of training, turn them into high-speed polo ponies. In addition to going fast, they've been taught to turn on a dime, ignore a swinging mallet, and appreciate tea with little cucumber sandwiches.

---

[1] Presumably in the more fashionable caves.

Here are the basics: There are four polo players per team. The field is 300 yards long and has a goal post at each end. You get one point per goal. The object of the sport is to ride around the field and knock the other team unconscious by hitting them with the ball (which is often traveling over one hundred miles per hour), the mallet, or just ramming them with your horse. I say this because I paid careful attention to "the worst hits of polo" segment of the video, which made motorcycle-racing accidents look tame. As far as I could tell, you're allowed to do more or less anything in this sport except trample an opponent more than once during a single play. Violation of this rule may cost you a tennis bracelet and a set of matching cuff links.

The game is played in a series of seven-and-a-half-minute rounds called *chukkas* (pronounced "chaka" as in Chaka Khan). Matches are made up of either four or six chukkas. Sometimes they just play as many chukkas as it takes until the goal total reaches twenty-two.

After each chukka, all the riders get fresh horses. So, for bigger matches, each player needs eight to ten horses. At around $50,000 for a top polo pony, you're looking at half a million dollars worth of "equipment" just to get into a game.

The big difference between an English and Western saddle is that the English model provides nothing to hold onto. The idea is that you're supposed to balance yourself and move with the horse's rhythm. I happen to know from prior experience that I have about as much horse-rhythm as a rubber doormat. So I asked John P. for one of his more docile steeds, perhaps one with a name like Old Gluestick. John P. agreed and put me on a high-mileage, one-eyed steed named Millie.

Millie is a very famous polo training horse. She was used to teach Prince William, the Sultan of Brunei, and several extremely famous British TV personalities I have never heard of. However, Millie was, at least in my opinion, far from gluestick status. She was about the best horse I've ever ridden. This may not say much for my riding experience, or perhaps it says a lot about polo-pony training. She was more responsive than a Ferrari, although she pulled a bit to the right and went noticeably faster when we were heading in the direction of the barn. Best of all, she positioned herself perfectly for me to take a swing at the polo ball when we approached it at high speed. Unfortunately, eight times out of ten I'd miss horribly, lose my balance, and end up clinging to Millie's neck as she galloped across the polo field. Hitting the ball is much harder than it looks—it's like trying to play golf out the window of your car while driving down the highway in rush-hour traffic.

Howard Hipwood, captain of England's national team for years and probably England's most famous polo player after Prince Charles, decided to show up and test ride a few ponies. John P arranged a scrimmage with several players, hoping to break in a few of his younger ponies at the same time. John P assured me that I had made tremendous progress during the day, but they weren't at this moment looking for a galloping-around-the-field-clinging-to-his-horse's-neck sort of player, although perhaps under other conditions (read: on another planet) this technique might prove useful.

So I just watched. The match was pretty exciting, although it was also pretty confusing. Teams switch sides after each goal, and I kept losing track of which team was supposed to be heading in which direction. I wasn't sure whether the players were making nice passes or total screw ups.

The other odd thing about polo, which I learned from a New Zealander who was also watching, is how the funding works. Since it doesn't attract big television coverage or lucrative contracts from horseshoe makers, top players make their money by playing with rich people, called "patrons." So you get these semitalented (or less) rich guys playing on competitive teams with the world's best players. You'd think it would make the pros feel like gigolos and the patrons embarrassed to have everyone know that they pay people to play with them. But apparently it doesn't. Imagine George Steinbrenner putting himself into the Yankees' lineup. Or Tiger Woods and David Duval partnering up with Bill Gates and Warren Buffett in the next Ryder Cup. Polo patrons pony up serious money: roughly a thousand dollars per match for each player they want on their team.

Despite the patron aspect, it's still a high-speed, action sport with exhilarating injuries that make for good spectating. And it looks like good fun to play. If it weren't for the expense, the "worst hits of polo" images flashing through my mind, and the minor fact that I can hardly stay on my horse, I'd be out having a chukka right now.

PART THREE

RELATIVELY HARD CORE

Ice Speed

Let Loose on Lillehammer's Luge Run

 LILLEHAMMER, NORWAY

LUGING. NOW HERE'S A GREAT SPORT. AT LEAST THE RULES are easy to follow: whoever squeezes into the tightest body-suit and can still manage to point their toes wins. Of course this is not the actual competition. The actual competition involves zipping down a frozen waterslide at the speed of Internet stock growth on a tiny sled that looks like two speed skates held together with a welcome mat and crushing opposition—sometimes by as much as 2/1000ths of a second. The reigning world champion is Georg Hackl from Germany, whose success might be credited to his streamlined profile, which includes the omission of several unnecessary vowels.

I can appreciate this sport because I used to love sledding as a kid. I had one of those red plastic sleds shaped like a giant contact lens. The beauty of this clever design was that there was no conceivable way to steer it. The only thing you could count on, was that the sled would turn you around backward and then, once you were off guard, guide itself toward the nearest tree.

When my parents determined I was ready, I received a rectangular plastic sled with quick-action dual hand brakes that, I soon discovered, were only effective for stopping the sled when the sled was already stationary. But the sled was ideal for jumping. My neighborhood friends and I spent hours building jumps that would sometimes launch us several inches into the air.

I took a break from sledding during high school, briefly resuming again during my freshman year of college, when—inbetween lofty intellectual pursuits—my fellow scholars and I would slide down the football stadium's hill on stolen cafeteria trays, making sure to tumble off at the last possible moment before colliding with an inconveniently placed cement escarpment.

You have to factor in all this background information to understand how I came to be sitting at the top of Lillehammer's $25 million Olympic bobsled track on a luge sled that looks about as easy to steer as a chaise lounge, though not nearly as comfortable.

I looked up at Asle Strand, Norway's two-time Olympic luger and former coach of the Canadian Olympic Team, for guidance. Asle, now forty-five and retired from both competition and coaching, handed me a helmet and told me to just lie back and keep my arms straight. He showed me how to turn the sled by using the insides of my legs to put pressure on the front rails. Unfortunately, this required the use of my inner thigh adductor muscles, which are very weak on account of the fact that at health clubs I refuse to sit in the adductor muscles machine—it looks very much like an OB/GYN examination chair and, when operated, exposes your private region in a very mature-audiences-only sort of way.

Asle told me I just needed to steer "into the turn and out of the turn." Of course, I had no idea how to steer into or out of the turn. Do you steer in the same direction as the turn or try to point the sled up into it? He told me to think of a high, left-banking turn like a left curve in the road with a straight stretch in the middle. I should turn left at the beginning of the curve, then go straight, then left again at the end of the curve.

"What if I hit the walls?" I asked, as Asle helped secure half a plastic Coke bottle to each of my elbows with brown packing tape.[1] I felt about as protected as a hockey goalie using a facemask made from a paper plate with two cut-out eye holes.

"You will hit the walls," he said.

"What should I do?" I asked, wondering if I should be pursuing this line of questioning at the starting gate with twenty seconds to go.

"Do what you have to do," he advised.

"And what is that?" I asked, pushing off.

"Survive!" he shouted after me.

I went into the first curve, oversteered, and slammed into the wall. Fortunately, about 1/100th of 1 percent of the impact was absorbed by the Coke bottle. The sled kept going, gaining speed as I began to tell myself that I had no business doing this, at least with my current insurance policy. I shot into the next turn, this time climbing the curved wall. Without enough speed, or perhaps faulty steering, I again rammed the bottom edge of the curve. My elbows and shoulders were aching and I continued to gain speed as I proceeded into a straightaway, where I seemed to go every

---

[1] This was meant to protect my jacket from ripping, not my arms.

direction but straight, ricocheting off the walls like a BB fired down a drainpipe.

After another turn or two I was going 55 miles per hour (virtual speed: 16,000 miles per hour) with the sled vibrating violently. I longed for my old saucer sled. In addition to lacking the metal rails that could become lethal during a crash, it would have had me turned around backward by now, sparing me the sight of the monster turn—its walls arching up like a frozen fifteen-foot breaking wave that was approaching.

The centripetal force held my head down, so I couldn't see when the turn was going to end and steer out of it. The sled (also called a *rodel*, not that it mattered at this point), up on one rail like the *Dukes of Hazzard* car just before a commercial. It came down a second later with a slam, bouncing my left leg over on top of my right, so that I was speeding along in what is known in the waterslide world as the "enema-prevention position."

I uncrossed my legs, popped through another few turns, and felt the sled slow as the track turned uphill. I was finished. I looked up, stunned.

"I'm not doing that again" were the first words out of my mouth.

I caught a ride in the support van back to the starting area to pick up the gear I had left behind. There I met up with other first-time lugers and learned about their crashes and bloody noses—information that might have prevented me from going down in the first place. Yet, everyone was taking another run. They were starting the neophyte competition. I couldn't back out now.

We started a little higher up this time and got a little more speed out of the starting gate. This ride was ever-so-slightly less traumatic, perhaps because I couldn't see much because of the falling snow obscuring my vision.

My time was 1:08. "It wasn't the worst time," Asle said at the end of the day. "But you didn't make rookie of the year, either." The winner of the competition clocked 59 seconds. The 9-second difference is like 27 luging years.

I must have forgotten to point my toes.

Kilimanjaro through the Back Door

A Hike up the Highest Peak in Africa

ARUSHA, TANZANIA

I AM LYING ON MY BACK WITH MY LEGS PROPPED UP IN the air, allowing the pus to drain from the seven infected blisters on my feet. (I'm not sure where they're draining to—possibly my head.) Along with a receipt for $585 and a few fuzzy snapshots, these festering vesicles are the only physical evidence of my trip up Mount Kilimanjaro, the tallest peak on the African continent.

The major difference between me and the thousands of other tourists who attempt this 19,340-foot mountain each year (aside from knowing how to spell the word *vesicle*), is that I was foolish enough to attempt it in rented hiking boots.

Most adventurers pay between $450 and $1,000 to climb Kilimanjaro; the price varies depending on the route, number of days on the mountain, and comfort level of the trip. The cheapest and most popular is the five-day Coca-Cola Route, thus named because the beverage can be purchased at conveniently placed rest huts along the ascent. But $1,500 seven-day trips are not unheard of. These involve upwards of eight porters per tourist and such luxuries as a separate dining tent, reclining chairs, and a portable Western toilet. I kid you not!

I opted for the Machame, or "scenic route," the second most popular ascent. This expedition takes six days, approaches the summit from the west, and takes the south face down.

I made my arrangements with a tout named Swali who works for the Arusha-based tour agency B. M. Travel. He was supposed to show up on the day of departure with all the gear he promised: a North Face Gore-Tex jacket and sleeping bag, Patagonia fleece and hat, Lowe long underwear, and just about every other outdoor brand-name product that comes to mind. There were also supposed to be glacier sunglasses and four pairs of hiking boots to choose from.

What he actually arrived with (several hours late) was—to the untrained eye—about $10 worth of hand-me-downs from the Salvation Army. I believe he had managed to put together the least mountain-worthy selection of clothing currently available in Tanzania: cotton sweatshirts, t-shirts, and a few ripped nylon pants and hats that most piss-drunk winos would refuse on a freezing night. He brought only one pair of boots. And the sleeping bag, meant for summer use only, was without a zipper.

Swali acknowledged the sleeping bag zipper problem and located another insulation-free replacement, but the boots, he asserted, were fine. And they would have been—for someone with slightly smaller feet. The rest I would have to live with if I wanted to start up the mountain that day. If I backed out, which was extremely tempting under

the circumstances, the extra day required to make arrangements with another outfitter would mean I'd miss my flight.

Jason, a twenty-six-year-old Englishman who at least
had his own boots, was in a similar position. So, with more
than our fair share of reservations, we set off to summit
Kilimanjaro with gear appropriate only for providing serious climbers with hours of amusement. My ensemble was
augmented by a rust-orange snowmobile hat, a pink re-
versible nylon jacket, and some aquamarine lycra pants that
could only have been purchased by a Frenchman; they
clung tighter than most designer jeans, and the fly was
sharp enough to draw blood.

The "glacier glasses" were made from the lightest shade
of plastic currently in manufacture. Cut-out pieces of a
Sprite bottle would have been more useful.

En route, we picked up John and Clair, a young
English couple. Apparently, they would be joining Jason
and me on our "private tour." At the drop-off point, our
guide, Lucas, sent us all ahead with a porter named
Tumaine (pronounced "Two-man") while he sorted out
the rest of the porters. He explained that we would require
two porters each—one to carry our gear and the other for
the tents and food. It seemed ostentatious. But after thirty
minutes of hauling my own gear with little progress while
others bounced ahead, I realized the futility of my prema-
ture decision and hired some porters.

The first five hours took us through a rain forest along
a mud trail over a foot deep in most places, each step making a comical, armpit-fart suction sound.

John, I learned quickly, was a loquacious twenty year
old. He had an entertaining, albeit totally irrelevant, quip
for everything. Herc are a few of my favorites: "I like bite-

size Snickers so much better than regular size"; "We should have a catapult on this mountain and shoot people into a net suspended in the clouds"; and "I'm going to see how many days I can go without changing my boxer shorts." I don't think he stopped talking for more than a few seconds during the first day, and he was drinking at the time.

With our packs coming up behind us, along with lunch, we only had two canteens of water and a few chocolate bars among the four of us. We finished off the water, thinking Lucas and porters would catch up, but they never did. Dehydrated, we pressed on, trying to reach the 10,000-foot camp before dark—unsuccessfully. It took an hour of stumbling up the pitch-black trail without flashlights, before we reached Machame Camp. The six or seven other, better-organized tours had already set up their tents and eaten dinner hours before.

When our gear and food finally arrived late in the evening (the porters had stopped for a rest and fallen asleep), we ate a quick meal and headed for the tents. I climbed into my sleeping bag, which was perfect...for a seven year old. It came up to my stomach. And that's only when it was half unzipped so I could squeeze my waist in. But the sleeping bag didn't get much higher than my knees because the porters—basically nice guys who clearly did not have the world's most desirable jobs—had set up our tent, a model that might have been cutting edge in the early '60s, on a slope that would have been better suited for skateboarding. The sleeping bag and everything else slid to the bottom of the tent. I slept with my hat, gloves, jacket, and shoes on and still managed to freeze. At around 2 A.M., with my teeth clacking like castanets, I cuddled up to Jason, and prayed he wouldn't wake up and notice.

The next morning began with our first view of the snow-covered summit; it was stunning, but farther away and steeper than I had imagined. Lucas explained that the top usually clouds up during the day and clears up by sunset. My eyes remained transfixed on the peak until it disappeared.

We only had a few hours to walk to the next camp, Shira, at 11,500 feet, where we would stay for two nights to acclimatize. A fairly tame itinerary so far. The bigger problems (and bigger blisters), I had a feeling, were still ahead.

During our two-day acclimatization at the 11,500-foot-high camp, we spent time with climbers from other tour groups. They hadn't paid much more than our $585 fee, yet they received two nights in a four-star hotel—at the beginning and end of their trip—airport transfers, and tents big enough to play racquetball in. Plus, their porters would bring hot water right to the doorway of their tents every morning so they could wash their faces. After washing, the discarded water would inevitably run down the small hill into our comfort-proof tents, which was generally how we woke up. In Kilimanjaro terms, we were roughing it.

Daytime was usually cloudy, but the clear night sky afforded us ample opportunity to stargaze. The view was magnificent, though I could never manage to see all those renowned constellations we spent most of our time looking for: bulls, crabs, hunters with designer belts, and so forth. I had enough trouble making out the kitchen appliances.

We took a short "acclimatization walk" with Lucas, who had two rather unique qualities. The first was that he almost never answered the question you asked him—which can get a bit frustrating when you're requesting vital information, such as where the toilet is (his answer: "The sun will set in about two hours"). Second, he always walked around with a little transistor radio. And since he was usually walking with us, we didn't experience much of the national park's serenity. Instead we heard everything from Ricky Martin to Bombay's latest Hindi pop hits through his tin speaker.

Of course, we were not without our own quirks. We relentlessly badgered Lucas about the altitude. "How high are we now?" we'd ask after every ten minutes of upward hiking. Occasionally, he'd even answer us. And sometimes with potentially correct information—meaning a figure that was higher than the one he told us ten minutes before.

Jason and I were cold, uncomfortable, and aesthetically offensive in our rented outfits. John and Claire, it turned out, didn't bring any real climbing clothes either. This was their first trip up a mountain, and they were under the impression that a few cotton t-shirts and a fleece jacket would be fine. Moreover, neither of them brought flashlights. I'm not sure if records are kept for this sort of thing, but I believe we may have been the least-equipped team ever to attempt Kilimanjaro.

On the fourth day, we set up camp at 13,200 feet, napped from 6:00 to 11:30 P.M., took a quick swig of coffee, and started making our way toward the summit in the dark. John and Claire stumbled along without flashlights on the rocky trail. About two hours later, the air became preposterously thin, nearly squelching John's banter, but not quite. Our heads began pounding. At this height, you could get oxygen deprivation from arching your eyebrows, yet this is when the trail became vertical. And Lucas, who suddenly admitted he hadn't taken this route for a few years, looked a bit lost to me.

We scrambled up loose rock to a steep, fifteen-yard-wide ice patch. Without a rope, ice ax, or crampons, it was a sketchy traverse. But we had none of these. One slip and you'd be seventy-five yards down the mountain with your head wrapped around a rock. I took off my gloves and tried to dig my nails into the ice for added grip. There were a few close calls, but no one took the express ride down.

After two more such crossings, we reached the bouldering portion of the climb. Shinnying up the rocks wouldn't have been a problem a few thousand feet lower, but at 18,000 feet our heads were spinning. I could hardly stand. Then the wind picked up, freezing the sweat in our cotton outfits.

"Only two hours more to the summit," Lucas declared, as we reached the rim of the volcano after four hours of hiking. My heart sank. "I thought you said it was four hours to the top." I mumbled, shivering and befuddled. He had clearly doctored the figures to make this route more attractive, but the only realistic way down from here was to press on to the top and take the Coca-Cola route

After two hours of stumbling like drunks up the sandy slope with nuclear reactor-like headaches, the summit came into sight. "Look, it's just up there! We made it! We're the first ones!" Lucas declared. And with that he gave me a hearty slap on the back, which knocked me over and sent me a few yards back down the mountain.

Miraculously, we reached the summit about ten seconds before the sun's first rays crept over the horizon. Exhausted, overwhelmed by the rugged icy surroundings, and mesmerized by the fiery red ball rising up before us, Claire began to cry. John, Jason, and I stood in silence, completely stunned, then grabbed our cameras and began snapping away.

After five minutes of summit euphoria, my headache and dizziness abated. It was suddenly all worth it. Nothing I had read about reaching the top prepared me for it, and I'm certain neither my laptop nor my camera can do it justice.

Fifteen minutes later, the peak began crowding with arriving hikers. It was time for us to head down. The lower we hiked, the more people we saw making early, altitude-sickness-related retreats. Seeing them turn back evoked an odd mix of sympathy and elation.

The punishment for our success, I didn't realize, was still ahead: a five-hour descent to a camp at 10,000 feet. It was, in some ways, more difficult than reaching the summit. As my feet and torso defrosted, my legs turned to rubber and my toes jammed into the front of my boots. By the time I reached camp, my blisters looked more like bullet wounds.

After a three-hour muddy limp to the bottom the following day, we were met at the gate by park rangers selling "Just Did It" t-shirts. It occurred to me that these were the first park rangers I had seen since I paid the $375 park entry fee six days ago—a fee that didn't seem to get farther than five inches into the park. There had been zero upkeep on the trail, no shelters for the porters, and no rescue stations (although part of this money is meant for rescue operations). In short, it's a joke.

But it was the porters who had the last laugh. When it came time to hand out the tips, there were two porters I had never seen before. "We needed these men to run ahead and prepare the camp," explained Lucas in dramatic fashion. This was a common ploy—Lucas and the others would later split the tips of our fictional porters—but for a whopping $10, who am I to make a molehill out of a mountain?

Till the Dhows Come Home

A Sailing Trip to African Islands

LAMU, KENYA

I'VE ALWAYS HAD A THING FOR SAILING. I GREW UP NEXT to one of Minnesota's 15,000 lakes (it says "Land of 10,000 Lakes" on the license plate, but that's just Midwestern modesty) and spent a number of my summers at sailing camp, learning how to tie knots, race other pubescent sailors (or simply ram them), and drop tiny, yet vital and painfully expensive, metal rigging parts, for which I was later billed, into the water.

So, for me, a sailing trip on a traditional wooden dhow seemed like the perfect contrast to three days of bouncing around Kenya's Masai Mara game reserve in a dusty Japanese minivan trying to spot wild animals hidden behind a ring of other dusty Japanese minivans.

From Nairobi it was just an overnight train trip to the coastal port of Mombasa, then a two-hour *matatu* ride (same Japanese minivan, but ten years older and filled with four times as many passengers) to Malindi, then a $30 flight north to the island of Lamu, where Signe and I landed at an airport with a terminal small enough to spit across. It was a thatched hut with a single podium check-in counter and a row of wooden benches. Funny, I thought, even in this remote spot the concept of a waiting lounge was already an anticipated aspect of air travel.

Lamu is perhaps best known as one of the jewels on the budget traveler's "Hippie Trail," set into the proverbial crown alongside the likes of Goa (India), Dahab (Egypt), Byron Bay (Australia), and Kathmandu (New Jersey). Locally, this island is known as an undeveloped Zanzibar, an ancient trading post with more Arabic and Portuguese influence than African. Although, with a casino on the way, a new four-star hotel, and the celebrity of royal part-time resident Princess Caroline of Monaco, this predominantly Muslim isle may catch up to Zanzibar soon.

The much-touted relaxed pace of the island, however, is eclipsed by much touting. No less than twenty locals, all trying to be helpful (read: earn a commission), compete to guide passengers to a hotel. We knew it would be difficult to bargain for a good hotel rate if the hotel owner had to pay off a "guide." So, after crossing the channel from the Manda airstrip on a diesel launch, we tried to lose them. We started by asking nicely, then begged them to leave us alone.

"Pleeeease," I implored, frustration dripping from each vowel.

"No," one of the touts countered, "this is how we survive. Would you rather we steal the money from you?" Odd that he saw these as his only two business options in life.

We stopped at a café for a fresh fruit shake, hoping they'd get bored and leave. It wasn't long before we discovered this was a bad move. The other touts finished escorting their toutees to hotels and were now able to devote their full attention to us—the last remaining visitors without a hotel.

As we left the cafe, a verbal battle erupted over who would take the commission from the hotel we would eventually choose. We staged a sit-in on the sidewalk, stating we wouldn't move until they left us alone. After ten minutes it became clear we weren't going to win this one—these guys had nothing better to do until the next plane arrived the following day.

We ended up dropping our packs at a $10 inn and then heading out, thinking the hassles would be over. Not quite. The same group was waiting for us to emerge so they could help us arrange (read: commission) a dhow trip to the surrounding islands, an almost obligatory activity for every passing globe trotter. The dhow is to the east coast of Africa what the felucca is to Egypt, the junk is to China, and the floating, discarded condom is to Manhattan.

After declining several pricey offers, we joined up with a nice Israeli couple who had found a boat and were looking for a few others to share the cost: $30 per person for four days, including snorkeling, fishing, and prepared meals. We were told we would head to four islands—Kiwayu, Paté, Manda Toto, and one nameless, uninhabited isle with a village that has never been visited by foreigners—all the while avoiding the Somali rebels in the area.

Captain Kelly, a soft-spoken thirty-five-year-old, told us to be ready to leave at five the next morning.

"Five?" I echoed, praying I wouldn't have to start relaxing at such a painful hour.

"Five o'clock Swahili time," Captain Kelly explained. "That's 11 A.M. your time. We start the clock when the sun comes up." For some reason, this method of timekeeping made more sense to me than starting the day American style: during the commercials between late-night talk shows.

First we had to get some drinks for the trip. And to do this, we needed empty beer bottles. Not to fill up, but to leave as a deposit. Bottles are so scarce here, the beer sellers can simply run out: bottle stock is much like the concept of cash flow in financial circles. This means there are always travelers running around begging locals for beer bottles—a fairly strange sight.

We set off on schedule, hoisting the triangular, patched cloth sail with wooden pulleys and riding out of town on a gentle breeze. Captain Kelly steered us through a narrow mangrove channel and into open water, where the winds picked up and we had to employ a wooden counterbalance to keep from tipping. This was handled by our two crew members: Mohammed, the ultraskinny twenty-six-year-old first mate who spent most of his time on "Planet Mohammed," a self-declared state of hash-induced euphoria, and second-mate Mohammed, a fifteen-year-old gnat-weight lad who never uttered a word and wore a hat made from the leg of a cut-off pair of jeans.

Mohammed and Mohammed lodged the thick, precariously narrow counterbalance beam into place, then climbed out onto it, leveling the dhow with their weight and providing a bit of speed—as much as you might hope for with a boat shaped like a Dutch clog.

At just about this moment, I needed to use the toilet in a seriously urgent way. And the way the toilet works on this twenty-foot-long open-hull boat is not entirely obvious.

So "going" goes something like this: put on a swimsuit, secure one end of a rope to the deck, take hold of the other end and jump overboard. Then it gets a little tricky because the boat is towing you along at pretty good clip. While trying not to think about the sharks in the area, you need to hold onto the rope with one hand, maneuver your swimsuit down with the other (being careful not to lose it entirely), keep your head above the rushing water, do your business, and hope that the wind doesn't suddenly die, leaving you in the middle of your business, if you catch my drift…or, perhaps, lack of it.

The sailing itself, however, was utterly enchanting. Part of the attraction of sailing here is the relatively calm waters—waves under three feet and wind that rarely overpowers the boat. After a full day on the water, we arrived at a secluded cove on Kiwayu Island.

However, it only felt secluded for about an hour. Another dhow arrived with two German travelers, followed by a crowded dhow with a family of Israelis and two Italians who complained they had been traveling by motor all day. Their dhow had a sail, but their captain didn't care for it. I felt sorry for them, especially watching them steam off the next morning, their engine rumbling like a fleet of Harleys in need of servicing.

We set off for a fishing village a few hours away on the island of Paté (pronounced "processed liver") that Captain Kelly claimed had never been visited by foreigners before. We beached next to a fishing dhow on a palm-lined shore, and the villagers rushed out to greet us. This "village" was comprised of just two families, although they had about twenty children between them. I don't believe I received a warmer welcome in all my travels. There was no TV here, no Coca-Cola, nothing but a few plastic buckets, which they used as drums. We sang and danced around a bonfire all evening.

As it turned out, we were the first tourists to visit …since a dhow full of Italians had visited them the month before, the lone English speaker on the island revealed. Unlike my previous experiences in eastern Africa, these families didn't expect a single shilling from us. They let us sleep under their partially thatched roof (and get ravaged by mosquitoes) for free!

As much as I enjoyed my visit, and as much as they seemed to, I couldn't help but feel torn upon departure. We didn't leave them any t-shirts or chewing gum, but this innocent exposure had somehow, in some small way, tarnished their isolated existence. It may take another 20, 50 or maybe 200 such visits before the effects (lack of interest in meeting foreigners and more interest in getting money from them) can be spotted, but this seems to be how the process begins.

As we headed around Paté Island on our third day, Captain Kelly still hadn't said more than a few words. However, when the topic of his love life came up, the prose poured from his lips. It turned out he had a long-distance liaison going with an American woman in Oregon, and he was seriously contemplating a move to the States. I asked how he'd get by once he arrived. We were all surprised to learn that Captain Kelly is anxious to drive a taxi—surprised because there's only one car on the entire island of Lamu. "From dhow captain to taxi captain," I said. He liked the sound of that.

Captain Kelly didn't want to stick around to see Lamu become a major tourist destination. Besides, the elbow of his steering arm was acting up on him. Signe, a doctor, diagnosed it as tennis elbow, gave him some anti-inflammatory tablets, and told him to try steering with his other arm for a while. Captain Kelly took the pills and advice only out of courtesy; he wanted us to stop at Paté Town so he could get some proper medicine.

It took over an hour to walk across the island to Paté Town, where we were met by the mayor, a rotund man in his late thirties who had a shiny watch flopping about on a metallic band four sizes too big for his wrist.

"Give me whatever you feel is fair when the tour is over," the mayor said, then walked us around town for an hour, pointing out relatively little. ("These are banana fields." "This is where some archaeologists were digging." "This is a stone wall.")

The town, he explained, was supposed to get electricity the following week, and everyone was busy getting ready for this "very exciting event." However, I can't say I witnessed any related activity during this tour—there was no one running around with lightbulbs or toaster ovens.

We stopped at the "traditional" doctor's house so Captain Kelly could get some real medicine. After taking a cursory look at Captain Kelly's dhow elbow, the doctor, a bald, robust man in his late sixties, prescribed some green leaves and told Captain Kelly to mash them up and put the paste onto his elbow immediately.

Back at the boat, Captain Kelly put the medicine on his arm and announced ten minutes later that it worked. He steered us off to the island of Manda Toto, keeping away from the mainland, where, he said, Somali rebels would be happy to rob us, shoot us, or whatever it is Somali rebels do these days.

On the way, an odd thing happened: An adult hippo popped out of the water about twenty yards off the port side of the dhow and started following us. We had no idea there were saltwater hippos. We also didn't use the "toilet" for a while after this sighting.

On Manada Toto, there were about ten young fishermen camping in thatched huts, and they let us share their shelter in exchange for some of Mohammed's hash. The Israelis, Signe, and I headed off to bed while the fishermen and Mohammed made their own cannabis cloud.

At around 11 P.M., Mohammed told us to get up and check out the rainbow. We were well acquainted with Mohammed's hallucinations by now, and we brushed off his invitation. He kept pleading with us until we finally capitulated. To our astonishment, there was, indeed, a rainbow in the night sky—a perfect arch of white light with faint colors illuminated by a full moon.

This was the image I held onto as we headed back to Lamu the following day, since the remainder of the trip was a bit of a drag. Literally. I had acquired, I later learned, bacterial dysentery and hookworm. Or, as this condition is known locally; dhow bowel.

Slip Sliding Away

Norway's Toughest Ski Race

LILLEHAMMER, NORWAY

THIS IS A DEATH SPORT. I'M NOT TALKING ABOUT kickboxing with golfing cleats. Or about Robbie Knievel trying to jump his motorcycle over the entire state of Nebraska. I'm talking about a sport far more dangerous—cross-country skiing! Someone just died from it, and not from boredom. In fact, during Norway's annual thirty-five-mile Birkebeiner race, one skier dies nearly every year. In this year's race I'm happy to report it wasn't me.

According to cross-country-ski aficionados (mostly Norwegian), the Birkebeiner is the world's toughest Nordic ski race. Its origins date back to 1205, when the Norwegian baby king, Haakon "Extra Vowels" Haakonsson, was skied to safety by Torstein Skevla and Skjervald Skrukka, the two best skiers in the Birkebeiner tribe of Norsemen.

The race route isn't exactly the same these days, nor is the equipment, but you are required to carry a seven-pound backpack, symbolizing the baby king—though no symbolic diaper changing is required along the way. Which is fine, because there's plenty to cope with already. Such as the first fourteen miles, which go straight up hill. And the 8,300 pairs of metal-tipped swinging poles racing alongside you, 85 of which belong to visiting American skiers.

These days skiing the Birkebeiner is a rite of passage for most Norwegians, up there with confirmation—a ritual most Norwegians think you should essay just once. The race organizers recommend logging in a total of no less than 200 miles before attempting the Birkebeiner. Most skiers train well over 500 miles during the season. Some ski over a 1,000 miles. I, on the other hand, managed to squeeze in just 100. Until three weeks before the race, I hadn't even tried skiing classic-style (no freestyle allowed). So most of my training consisted of running to the sporting-goods shop and buying equipment, then running back and buying more, until I owned nearly as much ski gear as the shop itself.

First I needed to decide if I wanted "plus" or "cold" skis, which refers to the temperature-related stiffness of the ski, not the nasal spray that should come with it. My skis, boots, bindings, and poles came to about $600, and that was just the beginning. This total didn't include the gloves ($40), hat ($30), socks ($20), ski rack for the car ($300), or the car to go under the ski rack ($20,000). And I hadn't even started skiing yet!

Then there's the ski wax. I could write an entire book on wax alone—although no one would buy it. And I would have to make most of it up since my knowledge of the subject is pretty limited.

Most of these wax products are made by a Norwegian company called "Swix," which is a fun word to say until you arrive at the cash register and find out that this word boosts the price by several thousand percent. (In Norway, ski wax can be purchased at most gas stations!) Sport shops keep the high-end Swix racing wax locked in glass cabinets next to the Oakley sunglasses because a tiny salt-shaker-size canister of it costs $120. I only wish I were kidding. The minute white wax granules could easily get mistaken for cocaine, and given the price, it probably wouldn't matter. If the Cali cartel ever decides to go straight, ski wax would be the perfect transition product.

Well, race day was upon me before I knew it, and I vividly remember jumping around nervously at the start in my slinky, borrowed, red one-piece racing suit. This is not an image one easily forgets.

Mostly I was nervous I wouldn't finish. I had filled my seven-pound symbolic backpack with various waxes, a Dave Barry book to remind me how silly this was, and Pat Conroy's *Lords of Discipline* to remind me that others have suffered and killed themselves for even more stupid reasons.[1] And a beer for the finish.

The start was divided into waves based on age and sex. People having the most sex went first. Well, not exactly. The older men started first, then the older women, and so on. My 1,000-skier age group started about two hours after the leaders. Which meant there was a better chance of me finishing dead last. Or, given the history of the sport, just dead.

The start was a mess of flying poles and people stepping on my skis. Fifteen minutes into the race, it gradually thinned out to about five lanes of skiers. In theory, the fast skiers were supposed to pass on the left, but this wasn't always the case. One guy skied into my lane while I was still in it and pushed me out.

---

[1] Also it was quite heavy, and helped meet the weight requirement.

Me: "Hey watch it!"

Hyper-Competitive Norwegian Skier: "I am skiing through. Get out of my shitting way!"

Me: "Stay in your own shitting track!

HCNS: "[Misused graphic insult]!!!"

Then he skied off. I picked up the pace and stayed on his heels. Literally. The front half of my skis were on top of the back half of his skis, so he couldn't get much kick. This is a totally cheap and sophomoric thing to do, but I have to confess it felt great. You don't see many fistfights in cross-country skiing—this is about as close as it gets.

Spectators lined most of the course, many cheering and some handing out drinks. However, a number of the spectators were enjoying their own drinks. And it was hard to tell if the plastic cups they were holding were for skiers or themselves. You don't know for sure until you grab the cup out of their hands on your way by and listen for some kind of reaction—or see what kind of drink you get. If it's scalding hot coffee, chances are it wasn't meant for you. I must have grabbed about three of these during the race.

The lethal aspects of this sport were becoming quite clear as the race progressed. If you keep going, you risk a heart attack. If you stop for long enough, you'll freeze to death. Then there's always the chance that you'll just suffocate on your own frozen snot.

About twenty-five miles into the race you come to the last incline, a five-mile killer. It has about four false peaks, and the mental trauma of realizing you haven't made it to the top must send hundreds of skiers to the psych ward each year. This is followed by a wicked six-mile downhill. The downhill death potential was something I had not even considered. After so many skiers had passed by, the tracks were icy and rough. This translates into high speed and no control. I figure I was going around thirty-five or forty miles per hour...until I wiped out. Luckily I rolled off into a snow bank and narrowly missed getting speared by the speeding masses behind me. I dusted off, made it another few minutes, then wiped out again. My legs were evidently too tired to manage some of the high-speed turns. Somehow my poles—about the strength of balsa wood—had not broken. And I needed them to double pole the few remaining miles (mostly uphill) to the finish in Lillehammer, since there were only about three cents worth of the $120 wax left on my skis.

I thought I was feeling terrible throughout the race. But I guess I was feeling less terrible than most of the other skiers. When I crossed the finish line at three hours and forty-one minutes—fifty minutes behind the winner, Norwegian national team star (and famous frozen-snot creator) Erling Jevne—I realized I had had the race of my life, beating my age-group target time (known as "the Mark") by nearly twenty minutes. I took off my symbolic backpack and reached past my symbolic literary support for my symbolic beer.

Little Big Horse

Pony Trekking in Lesotho

MALEALEA LODGE, LESOTHO

DOES PONY TREKKING IN LESOTHO SOUND LIKE A standard trip? It must, because every tour operator, travel agent, and guidebook writer outside the U.S. has already been through here, judging from the zillions of business cards that cover the walls in the Malealea Lodge bar. They've even plastered up some pony-trekking travel articles so we travel writers wouldn't have to start from scratch.

Apparently pony trekking in Lesotho is world renowned. I say this because one of the articles began "Sure everyone's heard of Pony Trekking in Lesotho...." Another piece went on for paragraphs about how brave the author was to embark on this trip, then outlined "how easy it is" for readers to arrange such a trip themselves. A third writer took the descriptive route and explained the color of every rock his pony had stepped on.

I hitchhiked to Malealea with a group of Germans in a minivan; upon arriving we made plans with Mick, the owner, for our own overnight pony trek for about $100 each. We bought our food at the only store.[1] I also purchased a Lesotho pony-riding hat for $3 right off the head of the hatmaker, complete with a year's worth of sweat stain. The main characteristic of this hat, other than its smell, was that it had a small knob on the top that made the head of whoever wore it look like a kitchen pot.

The next morning we met our two young guides, Clement and Izekiel, packed up the ponies, and headed off down the trail at the speed of teenage facial-hair growth. I must say that these ponies didn't look like the kind I sat on at the state fair when I was six years old. They looked more like small horses, which is just as well because one of the Germans, Martin, weighed about 225 pounds and he would have surely crushed the average pony.

"What's the name of my pony?" I asked Izekiel and Clement. They didn't know. They didn't know the names of the other ponies either. The ponies were simply numbers one through five. I was riding Number Two.

None of the Germans had ever gone riding before. Reiner, who was as close to *The Odd Couple*'s anal-retentive Felix Unger character as any German could possibly be, had a pony (Number Three) that went wherever it wanted, largely because Reiner wouldn't steer him, kick him, or raise his voice for fear of causing physical or psychological damage. Instead, Reiner would just pout until Izekiel or Clement passed by and led his pony out of the bushes.

After thirty minutes, we were supposed to descend a rocky trail into a beautiful gorge. Number Two did not want to carry me down the trail. Number One, Number Three, Number Four, and Number Five joined the strike.

---

[1] I want to say "the only store in town" but the store *was* the town.

We all had to get off and walk (read: drag) the ponies down the trail. Just as I wondered if we would be pulling them for the next two days, we reached a river; some six year-old kids rode and swam the horses to the other side while we were rowed across with the saddles in a boat made out of, I think, aluminum foil.

Once on the other side of the river, Number Two and the other ponies struggled up the steep trail to the first picturesque village, where we were met by the "friendly Lesotho villagers" who welcomed us with the warm greeting "Give me sweets!" Some also said "Give me money!" (No one said "Your head looks like a kitchen pot," but I knew they were thinking it.) We weren't too pleased with the tourists or travel writers who first doled out sweets and money to these people. But upon reflection, we figured if someone had handed out, say, electric waffle makers, we'd probably be hearing "Give me waffle makers!"

After we passed through the village, Karin, the lone woman on our trip, noticed that one of our guides had disappeared. "Where is Izekiel?" we asked Clement. Clement laughed. "Izekiel has girlfriend in village. He come soon. Don't worry."

By the time Izekiel caught up twenty minutes later, we had reached the next village. Again, kids ran up to us with smiles and the now standard demands. Again, they left disappointed when we didn't reward their begging with candy or money. And again, we left without one of our romantic guides, this time Clement. I was beginning to understand why we needed two guides.

We rode the ponies about eight hours before we arrived at the village where we were supposed to spend the night. But that wasn't the end of our first day's journey. We still had to hike for an hour to see a waterfall before sunset. Apparently, seeing the waterfall was the main goal of our trip, though this hadn't been explained up until now. Izekiel and Clement, whose extracurricular activities had left them exhausted, found us a local guide to take us to the falls.

We reached the scenic waterfall only to discover the sun had already set and the water was approximately zero degrees Kelvin. A few of us, who smelled more like our ponies than we cared to, jumped in and then hurried back to the village. After a beef jerky dinner we fell asleep in our *rondavel,* a basic round thatched hut with a mud floor. Ours was a VIP *rondavel;* we had glass windows, a gas burner, and some foam mattresses scattered on the ground.

We saddled up the next morning for our ride back, taking a slightly different way so Izekiel and Clement could rendezvous with two other girlfriends. We never managed to improve our speed much because Reiner had no more control of his pony on the way back than when he first mounted it. He was the sort of rider who wouldn't dare to nudge a rocking horse for fear he would upset it.

When we arrived back at the river, most of us decided to ride the ponies across ourselves, much to the disappointment of the six-year-old boys. We doffed our pants and rode the ponies into the water, which was deep enough in the center so that our ponies could just barely keep their heads above the surface. The saddle was completely underwater and I was beginning to wonder if I was drowning Number Two. Then I felt him touch the solid river bed. I have to mention this because it was the most exciting thing that happened on the entire ride.

Number Two and the other ponies marched us up the steep path they had refused to walk down and then we raced the remaining two miles back to the camp, or so to speak. The ponies had not gone faster than a slow trot during the entire trip, but, smelling home, and with a lot of kicking, they broke into a bouncy trot with occasional low-speed cantering (except Martin's pony, who was clearly straining under the weight, and Number Three, who had carried Reiner into a large bush).

I dismounted, wobbled into the bar with my genuine pony-trekking hat in my hand, and added my business card to the collection.

Reluctant Stalkers

Botswana's Okavango Delta by Boat and Foot

MAUN, BOTSWANA

SMACK DAB IN THE UPPER MIDDLE, SLIGHTLY EASTERN part of Botswana lies the Okavango Delta. This is not your basic delta because, as you may have gathered, the upper middle, slightly eastern part of Botswana does not lie on the ocean. Instead, the Okavango River empties into the middle of the Kalahari Desert, where it fans out and then gets absorbed by the sand, but not before attracting tens of thousands of large, thirsty African animals and tens of thousands of postcard-deprived tourists. In most places the delta canals are shallow, so a safari generally takes place in dugout canoes called mokoros, which can hold two people plus the poler, who stands in the back like a Venetian gondolier and pushes you through the marshy delta, only he doesn't sing or try to sell you a phony hat at the end of the ride. He just tries to keep you from getting attacked by hippos.

I hung out at Safari Island Lodge (a budget campground that is neither a lodge nor situated on an island) and eventually found some people to tag along with: a group of

Aussies, Kiwis, and Brits who were doing a three-day tour of the delta as part of their twelve-week Africa overland truck journey. They charged me $110 for three days.

A two-hour off-road ride in a Land Cruiser took us into the delta, where we met our mokoro polers. Mine was named Taba. He was about six feet tall and had negative body fat. He wore an oxford shirt, long dress trousers, and loafers—the least practical outfit imaginable for a safari.

As the eleventh person in the group, I had my own mokoro. After I got the hang of balancing, Taba guided the mokoro through the tall reeds with slow, relaxing strokes. We arrived at our campsite an hour later and set up our tents. That done, we told the polers we were ready to do some animal watching. They looked at each other and I couldn't detect what they were thinking. Then Taba spoke up and announced that we were going to look at some hippos.

We boarded the mokoros again and started cruising gently through the grassy canals, this time in search of hippos. After fifteen minutes, I realized we were taking the same route we came in on. When we arrived at one of the wider parts of the delta we had just passed an hour before, Taba announced, "*no* hippos" and we returned.

The following morning they said they were taking us to a special swimming area. It was the same area we went to see the hippos the night before. "You can get in now," Taba said. "What about the hippos?" we asked. "Don't worry, there are no hippos around here."

Back at the camp we learned that Island Safari Lodge had conveniently forgotten to mention that the water level in the delta was unusually low and there was only a single canal, which took only sixty minutes to traverse, deep enough for our three-day mokoro trip.

We spent the afternoon at the camp, were I finally got to spend some time with my fellow travelers. I spoke briefly to Bill, an Aussie who had just been at the Oktoberfest in Germany. I knew this because he was wearing an Oktoberfest hat, an Oktoberfest shirt, and Oktoberfest shorts, which seemed a strange thing to wear in the middle of Botswana. There was also Niki, a hairdresser from London who had on full makeup and jewelry; Rachel, a recent graduate from Cambridge Medical School who was completely hyperactive; and Sara, a six-foot-one-inch kickboxing masseuse from New Zealand. Steve, a thirty-five-year-old accountant, was the group photo expert. At least he looked the part, thanks to his tripod, massive zoom lens, and all-important fishing vest. His wife, Beth, helped carry some of his gear. They kept announcing how much they loved nature, but I couldn't help noticing they were constantly smoking and leaving their cigarette butts everywhere. The irony never occurred to them. It was hard to believe this random assortment of travelers had lived together for the last ten weeks on an overland truck.

That evening and the following day we went on a walking safari. I never bothered to read all the fine print in my insurance policy but I was pretty sure I wouldn't be covered for leopard, cheetah, or lion attack—especially if I was walking around, by choice, in a national park in Botswana during prime game-stalking hours. Amazingly, I was the only one in the group who was armed. I had a military weapon. At least the Swiss consider it a military weapon. I mostly use the little red knife for opening cans of tuna and slicing apples. I figured perhaps I could give the knife to a leopard as a gift.

Actually, there's an unarmed protocol for dealing with

all of Africa's creatures. If confronted by a buffalo, for example, you're supposed to climb a tree. If a tree is not nearby, you should run at a speed of at least twenty-five miles per hour, remembering to make continuous turns until you reach a tree.

Elephants are easily provoked, but they have bad eyesight—if you stand still they will think you are a tree or someone trying to act like a tree. If you decide to make a vertical getaway, choose your tree carefully: an elephant can push down a trunk less than two feet in diameter and then stand on your head.

If you are confronted by a lion, the idea is that you should, like a professional boxer, stare the lion down. In theory, it will run away. However, it might not.

If confronted by a leopard, the only thing you can do is pray.

As it turned out, we really didn't have to worry about finding game because Taba, who was acting as our guide, was, as far as tracking animals goes, a moron. He was walking downwind most of the time, which means that every animal within a twenty-mile radius could smell us coming. Also, everyone was yapping away, so if the animals happened to have nasal congestion, they could at least hear us coming. On the other hand, I was quite happy that we didn't stumble upon any of the animals we were looking for.

On the way out of the delta, a route I was now quite familiar with, Taba let me try my hand at poling. Almost immediately I swamped the mokoro, which was quite impressive since I managed it in only eight inches of water. It took me sixty minutes to get the hang of it, and by that time the ride, and the trip, was over.

The Fear of Gliding

Soaring on a Hang Glider in New Zealand

QUEENSTOWN,  NEW ZEALAND

THE MOMENT I SAW THE BROCHURE FOR TANDEM HANG gliding in my Queenstown youth hostel, I recalled my turbulent hang gliding experience in college. While studying for my final exam in vertebrate zoology (the study of large words), a friend of mine named Karen stuck her head into my room and said, "Doug, let's take a hang gliding lesson." Since I was cramming for a very important test, I insisted that we not leave until I had finished the sentence I was reading.

As we drove thirty minutes out of Colorado Springs, I had a few questions.

Me: "Is hang gliding the sport where they pull you around behind a boat with a parachute and bounce you off the Holiday Inn?"

Karen: "No, that's parasailing."

Me: "Is it the sport where you jump off a mountain with a rectangular parachute made out of wrapping tissue?"

Karen: "No, that's paragliding."

Me: "Is it the one where they strap you to an oversized kite and you jump off a mountain?"

Karen: "Yes."

Me: "Turn the car around."

But five minutes later we were each coughing up $40 for the two-hour course. After having been issued harnesses and well-worn hang gliders, we carried the gear up a gentle hill. The idea was that we would to run down the hill with our gliders, launch ourselves, and fly a few feet off the ground until we reached the bottom of the hill. Then we were supposed to start from farther up the hill and fly higher until, eventually, we would start from the top of the hill and achieve orbit.

That was the idea, anyway. What actually happened was that I ran down the hill with my glider, never actually left the ground, and felt monumentally stupid. On the second try, I ran faster, lifted off for a millisecond, ran a little more, flew a few feet off the ground, tried to readjust my altitude, and nose dived into the ground, swallowing six tablespoons of topsoil in the process. I repeated this several times until my mouth was fertile enough to grow a geranium. But the flying part never really blossomed.

Richard, the hang glider pilot in New Zealand, was my link to staying alive. So as we drove up the side of the mountain that we would be jumping off, I found I was becoming more and more friendly. By the time we got to the top, I was practically drooling on the man. "It's nice to meet you. Really! And that's a beautiful hang glider. I love the design."

Richard's hang glider was a flying advertisement for American Express. It looked like a giant credit card. And while these cards might be fine for buying a hang glider or covering any medical expenses I might incur from attaching myself to one, they don't instill much confidence as the means by which to achieve flight.

Richard explained what I was supposed to do: basically, nothing. Which was fine with me. "Just don't trip me while we are running during takeoff." Understandably, this would be a very bad way to start our flight off a cliff. So we practiced running together a couple of times.

Then he hooked me into the triangular crossbar, locked himself in, and radioed the nearby airport to ask them to clear some airspace for us. There was a glider in the vicinity, as well as a stunt plane, a helicopter, and a commercial aircraft which were taking off and landing regularly. Apparently hang gliders are at the bottom of the flying food chain.

"O.K., are you ready?" asked Richard.

"Yes," I replied weakly, now that I was standing ten meters from the cliff. We started running and, due to my over-concentration, I was still running well after we had left the ground. "You can stop running now," said Richard.

My mind tried to process the situation. I was lying on my stomach, several hundred feet off the ground, strapped to a piece of material the thickness of a Glad sandwich bag and hugging a man named Richard whom I'd only known for forty-five minutes. Why didn't I feel relaxed?

We circled around, looking for thermals, which is a hang gliding term for updrafts of hot air, or Mother Nature's flatulence. Thermals cause the glider to go higher, which provides a longer ride, which seems to be the main object of hang gliding. (Really good hang glider pilots can fly for upwards of thirty hours.)[1] To find the thermals, there was a Nintendo Game Boy-sized computer mounted on

---

[1] How they go to the bathroom is totally beyond me.

the crossbar that made annoying beeps whenever we gained elevation. Unfortunately, thermals are very small pockets of hot air, so to stay in the updraft we needed to make tight little circles that, after about ten minutes (and coupled with the beeping), made me extremely nauseated.

"Let's go straight for a while," I suggested.

"But," Richard pleaded, "then we'll start losing altitude."

"I don't have a problem with that," I said. When we straightened out, I began to enjoy the serenity and the scenery. But after a minute, this became too boring for Richard, who decided, for my enjoyment, to do a few stalls. He pushed forward on the crossbar, which drove the tip of the hang glider up, which made us lose speed until we had completely stopped in midair. Hence the name.

The exciting part came after the stall: The glider went into a nosedive.

"Richard," I said, trying to recover my stomach, which had moved up into my larynx, "have you noticed that we are about to crash into the fucking earth?!"

"Yes," he replied, "now watch this." And with that, he steered the glider into a sharp bank turn. Our solid nylon glider was no longer parallel to the ground, as it should be, but perpendicular to it.

"Try to relax," said Richard, sensing my firm grip on his back and now making a sharp bank turn on the other side. Richard put my hands on the crossbar and took his off, thus handing the controls over to me—as if that would help me feel more comfortable. I flew the glider for about ten centimeters and then, feeling just slightly underqualified, handed the controls back.

Richard brought us down safely after only two more stalls. As we approached the grassy field, we lifted our legs, arched our backs, and let the wheels on either end of the crossbar touch down.

Richard described our flight in relaxing, Zen-like terms. I would describe it as the sort of adrenaline-pumping experience one associates with taking a vertebrate zoology final exam after only fifteen minutes of studying.

Walking the Inca-Bahn

To Machu Picchu on Foot

CUSCO, PERU

TO MOST PEOPLE MACHU PICCHU IS AN ANCIENT INCA city that has been hidden in the Peruvian jungle for centuries. To me it is the name of a three-color toxic drink served in Cusco bars that I tried for journalistic purposes. It made me ill for two days, which delayed my trek on the Inca Trail—I refused to go by bus or helicopter.

Machu Picchu is the single largest tourist attraction in South America, but I didn't want to fight through swarms of tourists to see the ruins or trip over them on the forty-kilometer trail. So I went during the off-season, or rainy season as it's known in Peru. Initially I wanted to hike the trail alone to get a better feel of what it used to be like, but it ended up being much cheaper to go with a tour group, which included a guide, porters to schlep our food and tents, and a guarantee that we were somewhat less likely to get mugged along the way.

I was assured by the tour agency that there would only be twelve people in my group. And, technically speaking, there were only twelve in my group, not including Efrain, our guide. But it was hard not to notice the other two groups that started at the same time, walked at the same pace, and camped everywhere we did.

I was toward the rear of this large, multigroup pack when we set out on a dirt track that wound up the Peruvian highlands. Every time someone stopped to blow their nose or take a picture, we all rammed into each other, a sort of "fender bender" on the Inca Trail. After about three collisions I dropped back and tried to imagine that there weren't thirty-five tourists just ahead of me. My imagination was further impeded by the secondhand smoke left by several of the hikers and the small entourage from England who had found their way to the rear of the pack because they had to stop and accost their livers with shots of rum every fifteen minutes.

At the front of the pack were the Swiss. Andres and Marcello could have reached Machu Picchu in about two hours if they didn't have to keep stopping for the group. Michael, a German, was usually close behind them. He had by far the best personal hygiene in the group, opting to submerge himself naked twice a day in the freezing mountain streams we encountered.

The Swiss reached the campsite first. The rest of us straggled in over the next hour, with Johan, a Danish physical education teacher with influenza, bringing up the rear. The porters, mostly teenagers wearing sandals and carrying the equivalent of a Winnebago on their backs, came jogging in about the same time we did (having started an hour behind us).

At dinner we were entertained by Raoul, a Spanish surgeon who had memorized, in round numbers, 18 million dirty jokes. He spent most of the evening recounting them. Mayte, a Peruvian who has lived in Sweden for the last fifteen years, translated the jokes into English. Usually, however, she would start laughing hysterically at the punchline and it would take several minutes for her to calm down and translate it to the large group anxiously awaiting comic release.

On the second day we reached Dead Woman's Pass, which two politically correct Americans in the group pointed out should be renamed Dead Person's Pass. Johan, with his flu kicking into high gear, was the only one who nearly died going over it.

That night one of the Israelis became very familiar with one of the young Americans from California and everybody knew about it because, well, we were all sleeping in tents and we all had ears. They broke up the following day, perhaps because of the gossip, or perhaps seeing each other in daylight was enough. The other major topic of conversation was the Belgian couple who found each other through an ad in the personals and didn't seem to like each other's company but were sticking it out anyway.

On the third day the trail became the narrow cobblestone path through the jungle I had imagined. And it was mostly downhill—1,200 steps, to be exact. There were plenty of nice campsites around the bottom of the steps, but the guides felt obligated to help finance the Inca Trail's only hotel. We were all initially reluctant to have anything to do with civilization in the middle of our nature hike, but after we saw the Coca-Cola and Snickers bars, most of us were ready to trade our wallets, and even some minor organs, for them.

It rained that evening, so everyone slept on the floor of the lobby, except puking Johan, who spent the night decorating the bathroom, so to speak. It was still raining when Efrain woke us at 3 A.M. to eat breakfast and start walking the last hour and a half to a perch over Machu Picchu where we could watch the sunrise. We were assured that the sky normally clears by daybreak, so we all donned our rain ponchos, grabbed our flashlights, and headed up the slippery trail.

Naturally, when we arrived at the scenic overlook it was still pouring and we wouldn't have been able to see a fluorescent Inca refrigerator magnet dangling in front of our faces. So we descended into Machu Picchu to feel our way around.

Machu Picchu is an ancient Quechua word meaning "wear a silly white tennis hat." I say this because we immediately met the entire senior citizen population of Boca Raton, who had descended on Machu Picchu by train, bus, and helicopter. But not even their highly distracting presence could take away the excitement of arriving at our destination after a three-day trek.

We took a guided tour of the ruins, but afterward the guide told us it didn't mean much because there is no written record of Inca history. In short, he might as well have made everything up. We enjoyed listening to various Machu Picchu guides telling their groups totally different "facts," none of which could be refuted.

Guide #1: This is the Inca ceremonial bath.

Guide #2: This is the Inca water reservoir.

Guide #3: This is the Inca Jacuzzi and over there is Michael Jackson's room!

Some guides offered a spiritual tour. This is much more expensive, but it comes complete with crystals, cosmic chanting, and a certificate of accomplishment. Efrain didn't recommend it, but he said that (and another guide confirmed this) it had the Shirley MacLaine seal of approval.

Most of us were thoroughly exhausted by the end of the tour. The Swiss led the way to the nearby hot springs, where I soaked my feet, Johan regained his strength, the English polished off their rum, Raoul cracked some more jokes, and Michael, who had plunged into every body of water we had come across, decided that the hot spring was—possibly due to my feet—too dirty to enter.

PART FOUR

FESTIVALS

A Hat of a Different Color

A Day at the Ascot Races

LONDON, ENGLAND

I KNOW AS MUCH ABOUT HORSE RACING AS PAVAROTTI knows about long-distance running, Pope John Paul II knows about half-pipe snowboarding, or Tori Spelling knows about acting. But when the opportunity to attend the Ascot Races, one of England's premier social gatherings, came up, I felt I couldn't miss the chance to dress up like Little Lord Fauntleroy and spend a day rubbing elbows with royalty.

Once I put on my rented morning suit,[1] I found that I looked less like Little Lord Fauntleroy and more like a doorman for the Ritz Hotel.

To avoid glaring looks on London's Underground, I took a black cab to Waterloo Station. On the way, the driver explained that black cabs were originally designed with extra head room to accommodate people with top hats. For some reason, he wanted me to put my top hat on and test

---

[1] A morning suit is not a pair of flannel pajamas, as the name implies, but a gray-and-black tuxedo with a gray top hat.

the theory. But I didn't feel like putting on the hat because it made me feel like a world-class wanker.

"Really," he explained, "there's room to wear your hat." To humor him, I put it on for about three seconds.

"Yep," I told him, "it works."

As I stepped out of the cab at Waterloo, I saw about 300 men wearing my exact outfit. Suddenly, I was a member of this group of people I knew nothing about. And it looked like we were on our way to the prom.

Sitting next to me in my train compartment were Mr. and Mrs. Stiffupperlip Crustydrawers III. I accidentally made eye contact with the woman. So I smiled and nodded discreetly to cover up the inadvertent eye contact. To counter my nod and smile, which her husband had witnessed, she was compelled to say something trite. Such is the protocol at this level of society.

"Any tips?" she asked me, ever so politely.

Tips? Tips about what? I hadn't the faintest idea what she could have been talking about. "Tips?" I finally asked her after a rather awkward silence.

"Betting tips...for the race," she clarified, slightly puzzled. I could see her wondering if perhaps she was speaking to a total cretin.

"Ah, betting tips," I said, finally grasping the situation, "for the race." My American accent was now out of the bag.

"Yes," she confirmed, now with no doubt in her mind that she was dealing with an absolute ignoramus (from the New World no less), but bound by protocol to continue. "So, do you have any?"

"No," I said, then added "sorry" because the Brits seem awfully fond of insincere apologies. This seemed to do the trick. They could now ignore me without a bad conscience.

After an awkward hour on the train, I made my way through the front gate at Ascot and up to the first-floor balcony of the stands to check out the scene. From this vantage point, I could see the women's hats. Spectacular hats. One looked like an orange construction cone. Another looked like five cheerleader pom-poms tied together. Several looked more complex than nuclear detonation devices. Some were no bigger than a coffee cup. And some were more voluminous than the person wearing them—and could probably walk on their own.[2]

Then, someone announced that the Queen would be passing by in just a few minutes. About fifty professional photographers, all sharing this balcony, started frantically fiddling with their cameras. The only preparation I needed for my camera was to take off the lens cap, so, wanting to appear camera-competent, I played with some of the dials then struggled to return them to their original positions. I had a good place on the rail, and as the royal procession drew near, other photographers started pushing in on my space. I tried to box them out as best I could so I could get a decent picture, but they were checking harder than my intramural college hockey team.

---

[2] Few of the hats, I found out later, cost less than $150, which made me feel a little better about coughing up $90 for my morning suit rental, which, it turned out, I didn't need; a sport jacket and a tie would have been sufficient. The morning suit is only mandatory for men in the Royal Enclosure, an area so exclusive even member's polo ponies must have royal blood. And it's invariably filled with the extended family of Mr. And Mrs. Stiffupperlip Crustydrawers III and the haute-society types so tightly wound they haven't been able to pass gas since Churchill left office.

I got the Queen in focus with Prince Charles, Prince Andrew, and Prince Phillip sitting beside her. Suddenly, it hit me. Why did I even want this picture? It's not like there's a world shortage of royal family photos. No tabloids were going to pay me big money for this shot. I'm no paparazzo! I could hear shutters around me firing like Uzis. I paused, then I fired off a few frames. I just couldn't help myself.

After they passed, I took the pedestrian tunnel under the Royal Enclosure and made my way to the bookies. You can also bet the modern way with a clerk who operates a computer behind a window, but it seemed like more fun to place my money with one of the twenty or so bookies down near the track who make their own odds and scribble them on little backboards.

I settled on one bookie with a booming voice, composed myself, then tried out a horse-racing phrase I'd just learned: "Number four looks like he's on the muscle—think he's gonna get the distance if he doesn't leave it in the paddock." The bookie didn't have the slightest clue what I was talking about. Nor did I.

"So waz yer bet?" he finally asked.

"Number four to win," I said, handing him my £5 ($8), feeling more than a little daft. To my utter amazement, the horse won.

When I went to collect my winnings (about $12), I asked the bookie if he was getting a lot of action. "You mus be jokin'," he said. "Ascot sa wors toim uva yeh fir me. Got'll these richies eround, but noneuvum ah bettin' toips. Te busy drinkin', lookin' at tha 'ats, an bein' seen."

I went off to celebrate my victory with a beer. Only I couldn't find one. They were only selling champagne and wine by the bottle ($40 a pop!) plus an equally expensive pitcher of this blend of champagne and a liquid that looked like Worcestershire sauce. I begged the bartender for a small sample sip, then immediately wished I hadn't. It tasted like the champagne had been filtered through a well-worn hiking sock. And trying to clear my palate with the world's smallest $8 sandwiches didn't help much.

I spent the rest of the day milling around in my uncomfortably warm morning suit, looking at the elegant horses, the entertaining hats, and the champagne I couldn't afford. Next time someone asks me for an Ascot tip, I've got an answer: BYOB.

Vikings on the Loose

Attending a Little-Known Karneval in Sweden

LUND, SWEDEN

IN THIS PICTURESQUE SOUTHERN SWEDISH UNIVERSITY town, you can walk along genuine cobblestone streets, visit a medieval cathedral, and spot ancient Viking rune stones explaining how many early Vikings sailed to the New World and got knee injuries from playing on Astroturf. Once every four years, however, this historical hamlet is consumed by the Lund Student Karneval, and everyone is welcome to join in the celebrations.

The Karneval celebrates humor, denounces stodginess, pokes fun at its carnival status, and has been doing this as long as anyone can remember. Because Swedish is one of the languages that I butcher by trying to speak, I dove into this unique cultural event without much hope that I'd be able to tell you what it's all about.

What it's about, mostly, is drinking a lot of beer. Which is very expensive in Sweden. A round of drinks might set you back two entire checking accounts. Nevertheless, a good percentage of the people were so drunk for the three-day event they couldn't spell ABBA backward.

When I arrived at Lundagård, the campus quad that serves as ground zero for the festivities, I spotted a few of the mandatory vomit-inducing amusement-park rides and organic-food-free concession stands. Mostly, however, the quad was littered with white plastic wedding tents with see-through plastic windows. I went to check them out.

The first tent I entered was dedicated to the ideal sexual ritual. I gathered this because, in Swedish, the sign read IDEALSEXUALRITUAL. Quite extraordinary, I thought, that the Swedes have one word for this. And I would have felt like a real pervert waiting in line to go in if it weren't for the fact that the line was already about thirty yards long and filled with equal numbers of curious men and women.

Once I paid my $2 admission, I entered and was immediately confronted by the "sex oracle." Dressed in swami attire, hc had me stare at a bathroom plunger and tell him my thoughts. I told him I was afraid. He asked me what I was afraid of. I said I was afraid I had just paid $2 to stare at a bathroom plunger.

He concluded from this that I was "undersexed" and sent me to the next room in the tent, where I was greeted by a woman who told me to say *nej* ("no"), no matter what happened. Then she led me into the bedroom section of the tent, where there was a man and two women in their underwear. My guide sat me down on the bed with them. The women rubbed me on my chest and told me in very sexy voices to just say *ja.*

"*Nej,*" I said, very unconvincingly. I was quickly pulled off the bed and through a hallway where, while I continued to walk, a woman wearing a leather jumpsuit gently whipped my butt while a man in leather pushed a squirt gun against my nipple and pulled the trigger. It felt like an S and M car wash.

Next, I paid $2 to enter the environmental tent. Here, the focus was Oscar, a massive oak tree that went up through the middle of the tent. Once the three organizers got about fifteen people into the tent, they had us give Oscar the Tree a group hug. While we were embracing the tree, they played some police sirens and simulated a raid on us "environmental activists." As the siren grew louder, they chained us to Oscar and had us chant our commitment to the environment in Swedish, then instructed us to sing "We Shall Overcome."

After five minutes, we were released and, in return for our environmental commitment (and $2), we each received a green ink stamp on the forehead on the way out.

I wandered next into the massage tent, staffed by physical therapy students. After another $2 investment, I was led to a massage table where three women were waiting for me. The sign over my table read: ROBINSON MASSAGE. I had no idea what this meant, but apparently I had to get undressed for it. Once I was stripped down to my underwear, they had me lie down on my stomach. The women then covered me with enough lotion to lubricate a diesel engine and began rubbing. They spent a good portion of the ten-minute massage coating my "rumpa" with lotion.

On the table beside me was a guy in his underwear who was roped to a table and getting semi-gently pounded on by four masseurs. The sign over his bed read BRUTAL MASSAGE. Although awkwardly stimulating, mine seemed much more enjoyable than the Brutal Massage or the Jesus Massage, where the massaged party gets stripped to the waist, strapped to a wooden cross, blindfolded, and pelted with juggling balls painted to look like rocks.

I was told that this Karneval had fewer practical jokes than previous years. One tent reportedly advertised "Watch *Dallas* Backward," then after people paid to go in (presumably to see humorous video scenes played in reverse, with Larry Hagman appearing to spit up his scotch), they only saw a salad sitting on a table.[1]

In another tent, they brought in paying customers from two entrances on opposite sides of the tent and sat them facing a curtain in the middle. Someone announced the show would begin, and pulled back the curtain. Both audiences sat there and looked at each other, each thinking the other audience were actors ready to start the show. It usually took ten minutes for everyone to figure it out and leave.

The 1998 Karneval didn't offer many dull moments, but throughout the three days of festivities, it was hard to appreciate the historical richness of Lund. Most of the city was engulfed by the Karneval in one way or another—people puking on the ancient cobblestone streets, passing out next to the medieval cathedral, and tripping over the rune stones, getting knee injuries of their own.

---

[1] Dallas is understandably more difficult to spell backward than ABBA, so even many of the sober visitors left without discovering the joke. Also, it's worth mentioning that "salad" is spelled "sallad" in Swedish.

Running of the Idiots

Watching the Carnage at Spain's San Fermín

PAMPLONA, SPAIN

You can do a number of things to maintain your health, and avoiding Pamplona during the running of the bulls should cover most of them. This weeklong fiesta, better known in Spain as San Fermín, is an insidious combination of frat party, rodeo championship, and international track meet.

The first thing I noticed when I arrived at the train station in Pamplona was that everyone in the whole town was wearing the traditional San Fermín outfit: a white shirt, white pants, a red sash around the waist, and a red bandanna around the neck. It looked like Pamplona had been invaded by Pizza Hut delivery men.

I wanted to check out the *encierro* (the actual running of the bulls event) the next morning at 8 A.M. The bulls run every morning during the fiesta as part of their daily training regimen. Actually—and this is the complete truth—none of the intoxicated spectators I asked could tell me why the bulls ran through the streets. The best I could figure, it's a promotion for the bullfight that evening, not unlike running Mike Tyson through the streets of Las Vegas before a fight.

To get a feel for the event I followed local custom and stayed up all night partying in twenty different bars around town.[1] The nocturnal part of the fiesta worked something like this: everyone went to the supermarket, bought a liter of beer for $3, and chugged it to establish an alcohol foundation. Then they went from bar to bar, dancing and buying little cups of beer for $2 until they had no money left or passed out on the floor of the bar.

Every ten seconds an impromptu parade would go by. Parades of various forms, lengths, and sizes danced through the crowded streets all night, from high school marching bands to a lone drummer running down the street wearing the ever-popular fragrance: Three Liters of Beer Dumped on My Head.

At the height of the nocturnal fiesta, an unusual activity took place: crowd diving. This is just like regular diving, only there's no diving board, no pool, and no water, making this sport considerably more difficult. The object is to climb up something, let go, and drop into a crowd of people who don't seem to be entirely fond of playing the role of crash pad.

By 5:30 A.M., if they could still stand, people started looking for good places along the street to watch the bulls run. By 7 A.M., when I arrived, most of the best spots had been taken. Fortunately, I found a perch near the end of the run available only to the local TV crew and Americans carrying fake, but very realistic looking, press ID cards purchased in Bangkok for $3 each.

---

[1] Ah, journalism!

The first runners reached the bullring in a sprint. These runners, exclusively tourists, had apparently created their own event: the running of the bulls footrace. About the time they arrived, a rocket was launched from the city hall to indicate that the bulls had been released. Then the 1K fun runners passed by. Most of them were jogging leisurely because, unless the bulls jumped into a Formula One race car, there was no way they were going catch up. From what I could tell, about 70 percent of the runners never got within 400 meters of a bull, a fact they may have forgotten to include when retelling this event to their friends.

Toward the back of this second pack were little bursts of frenzy caused by people who thought a bull was behind them. They would run like mad right into the person in front of them, who, in turn, either ran faster or fell down and got trampled. The third group (10 percent of the runners) actually ran slightly ahead of, alongside, or under the twelve stampeding bulls, each of which weighed over a thousand pounds. Six of these bulls had been castrated and were supposedly non-aggressive, though it wasn't easy to tell which ones these were.

Ideally, the goal, other than surviving, is to place your hand on the back of a bull and run alongside him. The second coolest thing to do is to take a rolled-up newspaper and smack the bull on the head. Not surprisingly, the only prerequisites to join the *encierro* are being over eighteen and having an IQ that doesn't surpass your age.

While I watched, a Pamplonese journalist from a local TV station leaned over and shared some bull-running technique. "Everyone knows that if you fall, you should just stay down, cover your head, and let the bulls jump over you." Never ever, not even if Ross Perot becomes president of

Germany and bungee-jumps off the Reichstag, should you try to get back up before the bulls have passed. Unfortunately, not all the runners seemed to be aware of this basic rule. Few get killed, but almost twenty-five people sustain injuries every day of the fiesta.

Running with the first two groups seemed pointless. Running with the third seemed psychotic. I decided to give the *encierro* a miss. But not before witnessing one more San Fermín tradition.

For just a few bucks, you can enter the bullring stadium, the official finish line of the *encierro*. The bulls are immediately led out the other side of the stadium by matadors dressed in street clothes, leaving the bull runners milling around the large center ring. Then an amazing thing happens. They release a young, 3/4-size bull into the crowd. Hundreds of runners, armed only with their hangovers and a pair of Nikes, attempt to stay out of harm's way.

It was like watching the Romans feed Christians to the lions. Except these macho lunatics had volunteered. In ten minutes the bull had rammed about fifteen people. And when he started to slow down, they took him out and brought in a fresh one. The runners could climb out of the ring whenever they wished, but most never did. In fact, a small, courageous group sat down in a tight mass in front of the bull's gate, hoping that the bull would instinctively go around them. He did. But occasionally the bull, who had been fed so many steroids and growth hormones that he had no idea what his natural instinct was supposed to be, plunged right into this crowd.

Twenty seconds later, they unleashed another bull and things really got interesting. People would jump out of the way of one bull, only to get flattened by the second.

Human dodgeball. No one seemed to be seriously wounded—just bruised, cut, and humiliated. The crowd, who had paid $3 each to watch this spectacle, got their money's worth. Unlike at regular bullfights, this crowd was cheering for the bulls

Four exhausted but satisfied bulls and fifty injured tourists later, the event came to a close. I and about a thousand others decided to take a short nap in the public park. I woke up that afternoon, exactly twenty-four hours after I had arrived. I had grass in my mouth, strange smells on my t-shirt, and a silly red bandanna around my neck. Unlike a few of the people around me, at least I didn't have a bull's horn in my leg.

Takes One to Samba

Parading in the Brazilian Carnaval

RIO DE JANEIRO, BRAZIL

My feet are gold. Not a nice, tennis-bracelet gold, which might actually look okay on a pair of feet, or Goldfinger murder victim. Mine are more faded 1970s-dying-to-be-reupholstered-kitsch-lobby-furniture gold. This doesn't happen to everyone who dances in Rio's Carnaval...I believe it's just me. (More on this later.)

If I commanded you to give up meat, dessert, and alcohol for forty days, what would you do? I mean, after you punched me in the nose?

Enter Catholic Church (stage left) who gave the largely Catholic Brazilians this very order, citing Lent. ("Hey, look! Lent!") Since the Brazilians couldn't exactly thump the church officials, they took a more positive approach. "No meat, dessert, or hooch for forty days," they must have said, "My God, we've got to throw the biggest blowout party the world has ever seen. We need to chalk up forty days' worth of sinning to atone for, and the sooner we get started the better. Marco, you make some costumes. Miguel, see if you can round up all the booze in South America. And Maria, try to coerce some of your friends to come topless. Okay now, let's get cracking."

And thus, Carnaval was born.

Each year, Rio de Janeiro spends hundreds of millions of *reals* on the Carnaval, a production that makes the Super Bowl halftime extravaganza look like a dress rehearsal put on by a bunch of sixth graders at an overnight camp in North Dakota.

Visitors come from around the world to photograph the exotic costumes, sample the regional cuisine, and exchange warm greetings (and sexual diseases) with the locals.

I decided to go this year mainly because I was granted special permission to wear a ridiculously large costume and dance in Rio's big Carnaval parade.

I wanted to get to there early so (1) I could learn how to samba; (2) I could learn the words to our samba–school song; and (3) I could go to the beach the first day, forget to put sunscreen on my back, and get totally burnt while reading a good book, then lose about three pounds of dead skin two days later.

Rio's tourist bureau gave me a contact at the Mangueira Samba School, arguably the best in Brazil. Reinaldo, a radiantly happy, stout man in his thirties, was supposed to "tell me everything I needed to know." Evidently, he didn't think I needed to know very much.

"How many people are parading with the Magueira Samba School?" I asked him.

"Many."

"Thousands?"

"Many thousands."

"How many thousands?"

"Many."

This is largely how our conversations would go. And usually we'd have these information sessions while conducting Reinaldo's preferred method of Carnaval preparation: drinking *caipiroscas*.[1] These make Long Island Ice Teas feel like Shirley Temples. After just one or two, I'd forget my questions—my body would be concentrating on more vital functions, such as remaining upright in the chair. "Well, that's enough for today," Reinaldo would conclude. "See you here again tomorrow, right?"

The energy for Carnaval builds all year, especially the final few weeks. With only three days to go, it feels like the city is about to explode. The streets are filled with small parades called *bandas,* complete with drums, horns, singers, and sometimes an entire truck to carry the 900-gigawatt amp and concert speakers.

Some of these *bandas* involve more dancing, some involve more marching, and some have more drag queens than you can shake…well, maybe you should think twice before you start shaking anything at them. But they're full of *cariocas* (locals) and a small percentage of tourists, and you can easily jump into any of the *bandas* and parade along.

In the haunts near the Carnaval activities, I got a shocking dose of hospitality. One well-to-do couple was ready to hand Signe and me the keys to their now-empty beach home after five minutes of small talk at a beachside cafe. "We'll call the housekeeper and arrange everything, just say the word," the man (whose name I never even learned) said, picking up his cell phone. A couple on the

---

[1]   Derived from Latin; *caipi* meaning "a big glass full of" and *rosca* meaning "vodka."

other side of our table whom we hadn't even met countered with an invitation to stay at their empty beach home farther north in Bahia. It was all a bit overwhelming.

Two days before Carnaval I went to one of the Mangueira rehearsals ($8 to get in), thinking I'd learn the song, the samba, and the special hand motions to go with it.

Nope.

In a room the size of a high school auditorium, a few thousand of us listened to the Mangueira theme song played about two hundred times by a live band. Thanks to the state of the sound system, I couldn't make out the words. And there wasn't anyone showing us the Club Med-like hand motion, or samba footwork. Some of the people in the crowd knew it, but they weren't always doing it, and it was hard to see them. Every time I told Reinaldo, "I really think I should be learning the samba," he'd say, "Don't worry. You can learn later. It's easy."

Well, the samba does not look easy. It looks like you need to wiggle your feet and—here's an easy Portuguese word to remember—*bumbum* at the speed of quantum-neutron particle collision. (Note to physicists: I just made this up.)

"A samba school," the receptionist at my hotel finally set me straight when I returned at 3 A.M. frustrated at my inability to pick up the dance, "does not teach people how to samba. Think of it more like the Rose Bowl Parade Committee."

Next I dropped by one of the big pre-Carnaval balls at the Scala Auditorium. It was a lot like the rehearsal, only it was more expensive to get in, people wore tighter clothing, there were more couples making out than you'd see in the parking lot of a 7-Eleven adjacent to a high school, and I saw a multitude of surgically/hormonally adapted transsexuals (some of whom were topless—which, I might point out, is not something you see every day in my line of work).

With the clock ticking down to my Carnaval parade debut, I walked up to a few of the better dancers I spotted and asked them to teach me how to samba. "It's easy," they'd say, "just go like this." And they'd cut loose, gyrating their *bumbum* at hummingbird speed. I tried for hours, then finally developed a rather impressive samba technique …provided you think it's impressive to look like you're having a grand mal seizure on the dance floor.

Before attending Carnaval, the only photographs I'd seen from this event showed…well, you know what kind of photos I'm talking about: women with less fat than you could find at a vegan restaurant wearing little more than their tan lines and being supported by—according to my wife—plastic surgery.

In Brazil, you get an even heavier dose of these pictures: full-flesh coverage on the evening news and front-page spread in the newspapers. The special Carnaval section of *Caras,* the Brazilian celebrity tabloid, printed forty-eight photos of scantily clad women and only eight of men, people in costumes, floats, and musicians…combined. I counted them myself—twice! Of course, the statistic you men want to know is where you can get one of these tabloids and how much is a subscription to a Brazilian newspaper.

These pictures give the impression that Carnaval is made up of battalions of near-naked women gyrating down the street. In truth, there are far fewer than most publications would have you believe—about one for every five hundred fully costumed dancers and musicians by my rough estimate.

I now understand the root of this misconception. During the parade I spotted about twenty-five "photo-journalists" (including a few who weren't even holding cameras) hovering around each of these women, largely ignoring everyone else and trying to take pictures from angles that would be too racy for MTV.

Even the foreign print journalists crammed into the tiny press booth were discussing it. "Is [so-and-so] going to be topless this year, or wearing body paint?" I heard one man ask his colleague. (For answer, watch the 10 o'clock news.)

This sort of female exposure gets a bit more respect in Brazil. At least that's how it was explained to me. Take, for example, the rather unorthodox biography of one of the unclad dancers, Nilza Monteiro, found in the Carnaval program: "Nilza has been a journalist for ten years and has lived many years in Ribeirdo Preto, where she even had her own tabloid newspaper and worked on the Globo regional news broadcast...she has posed twice for the cover of *Playboy,* and was even elected by the magazine as having 'the cutest ass in Brazil.'"

Nudity aside, Carnaval is an absolutely stunning spectacle, and I promise you'll be exhausted by the end of it. Mostly because it starts at 7 P.M. on a Sunday, and lasts basically forever.

The party erupts as "students" from seven samba schools parade through the Sambodromo, a 60,000-person-capacity stadium built on either side of what looks like a 750-meter-long airport runway. After a few fireworks and a conversation-halting, Uzi-like burst of firecrackers, each school (with 3,000 to 5,000 participants) enters the Sambodromo and spends an hour filtering through its famous corridor while being cheered on by the spectators.

A dancing sanitation crew sweeps up, everyone takes a twenty-minute break, and the next school starts. The whole shebang goes until about 5 A.M., at which point 60,000 people attempt to return to their hotels in a total of five taxis.

The following night brings more of the same thing (but different) with the second set of seven samba schools.

Tickets range from $60 for nosebleeders to several hundred for a box seat. My press badge admitted me to both the packed, sweaty press box and the "journalist passageway," a 100-meter stretch of sidewalk along the parade where you can reach right out and pluck feathers off the costumes of passing revelers (not that I tried this…much).

I spent most of my time watching from the passageway, but the problem here was that the security wouldn't let me stop to watch unless I was busy writing something. I doodled in my notebook for nearly ten hours. Standing next to me were about thirty correspondents from around the world utilizing the same mature journalistic technique.

One of the most surprising aspects of the Carnaval was the samba-school songs. In Lund, Sweden, the last place I had celebrated a carnival, most of the lyrics were along the lines of "Let's get really drunk" or "Let's get really drunk right now." But in Rio, the themes were surprisingly poetic and profound. They sang of liberation from slavery, respecting native traditions. Think "We Are the World" sung in Portuguese, played with samba drums, and choreographed with topless dancers.

I absolutely can't forget to mention the *carros allegoricos*—the giant, wedding-cake-like floats that, prior to their debut, are as carefully guarded as America's Cup keels. Each float is professionally engineered, assembled by artisans and garnished with beautiful people. They emerge from the darkness at one end of the Sambodromo and disappear into the darkness at the other end. The spectacle is mind-numbing.

One of the floats getting the most press coverage carried a woman who had supposedly just given birth to an extremely realistic-looking baby that was (how fitting!) made entirely of silicon.

But I was most taken with the costumes. (Really!) There were legions of men and women dressed like frogs, camels, fish, Amazon natives, robots, aliens, pieces of kitchen furniture, and women in large hoop dresses called *baianas* spinning their way down the Sambodromo like whirling dervish initiates.

Each costume was the most elaborate, expensive-looking thing I'd ever seen...until the next one came along. From afar, the dancers looked like one semiorganic mass—a giant, sweaty, pulsing serpent of glitter, feathers, and plastic surgery—sort of like Zsa Zsa Gabor.

I was also watching the costumed dancers for another reason. I was trying to figure out what, exactly, they were doing, technique-wise, because in less than twenty hours I would be dancing along the samba runway myself. And I still hadn't the slightest idea how to dance the samba, sing our song, or do the hand movements. I was desperately hoping for some tips that might help me fake my way though—especially since silicon was out of the question.

And thus it went until an hour before my school's appearance in Carnaval, when I showed up at the staging area with my costume in two giant trash bags (I had no idea how to put it on) and realized I had much bigger problems to face. But I'm getting ahead of myself.

Let me backtrack and remind readers that this parade is a heated competition, with fourteen samba schools vying to be the pride of Brazil. I should also remind readers that these samba schools are not Arthur Murray dance salons but teams representing districts of Rio.

Each hour-long defile is judged on a variety of criteria, including *bateria* (percussion), *samba-enredo* (theme song, *fantasias* (costumes), and *belisa de plastico* (plastic surgery). Even reaction from the crowd is factored in.

The Sambodromo staging area feels like you're backstage at a Mel Brooks production. People were wandering around half-dressed in preposterous costumes, talking casually, smoking, and drinking beer.

A handful of women were running around in Brazilian-style bikinis. Brazilian-style is a cultural way of saying "not much." It's as if a regular bikini wearer said, "You know, I feel like I'm being a bit selfish with my swimwear. This bikini easily has enough material to make at least four or five swimsuits." So the tops are two lamé postage stamps held up with dental floss. The sequined bottoms, or what's left of them, seem to just disappear in a manner known in medical circles as a "wedgie." Not that I was paying much attention.

When I finally spotted my group (several hundred people with the same $250 costume), I pulled the outfit out of the bags and began to piece it together. First, I had to discreetly slip into the standard-issue "tighty whities." Over these, I pulled on a pair of lace bicycle shorts. Next came the tinfoil dog collar. (Please don't try to imagine this just yet.) Then a ribboned, tinfoil armband and this thing that's worn like a beauty-pageant sash, except it's about five times bigger, made of plastic and tinsel, and has silver streamers dangling from it.

My favorite part: an extra-large-pizza-sized wicker shield, which would come in handy if anyone started firing wicker arrows at us.

There's more. I haven't yet mentioned the hat—as wide rimmed as a Mexican sombrero and five times as tall, white and gold with giant, pink-tipped ostrich feathers protruding about two yards upward. The thing weighed five pounds more than my head, and keeping it aloft for any length of time requires neck muscles much bigger than mine. The only way to see my face would be to stand under the hat with me. Think Liberace meets the Three Musketeers and you won't be far off. According to Signe, it was the most hideous costume in the entire Carnaval. Quite an honor.

The other people in my group were, for the most part, tourists. I met a guy from California, a couple from France, an entire contingent from Japan, and there must have been at least thirty Brazilians from São Paulo. How had they gotten their costumes and permission to dance? Apparently this can all be easily arranged by the upscale hotels in Rio as late as a day before Carnaval begins for a few hundred dollars, the price of the costume.

There was just one minor problem. The costume people had forgotten to include my gold-plated sandals. When I pointed this out to one of the Liberace-Musketeer leaders, I quickly realized that it was not a minor problem at all.

"I'm sorry, you can't be in the parade," he told me. I thought he was kidding. "The samba school will lose points," he said quite seriously.

I pleaded with him to locate some sandals, and a phone call was finally made. After conferring with his colleagues, he explained that if they couldn't locate any shoes I wasn't dancing, end of discussion.

I couldn't quite grasp how they would lose points for such a minor detail but not for neglecting to teach me to samba or helping me learn the song.

As I was standing off to the side, waiting for the gold sandals, one of the Brazilians from São Paulo whispered, "They won't find any sandals. Just jump into the middle of the pack and hope they don't notice." So that's what I did.

Unfortunately, they noticed.

They had come to inform me that they couldn't find any sandals, and they were quite upset to find me hiding in the middle of the pack.

After this, of course, I snuck back into the lineup. And, of course, they found me again.

Two minutes to go and no gold sandals. I was sweating like mad in the 85-degree evening heat. And, I might add, I was pretty upset.

The customary barrage of fireworks went up, a cheer rose from our ranks, the *puxador* started singing, and the *bateria* kicked in with a beat that made my gall bladder oscillate.

Just as my group started walking the fifty yards toward the Sambodromo without me, a man came running up with a can in his hand.

"*Jeitinho Brasileiro*" (clever Brazilian solution), he yelled. "Take off your sandals!" he yelled.

I did. He spray painted them gold. I slipped them back on. He gave them another spritz for good measure. With wet paint oozing between my toes, I caught up with my group just as they entered the Sambodromo.

With the journalists, staff, and ticket holders, there were nearly 100,000 people lining the 750-meter-long Sambodromo. It feels, I imagine, something like being in the opening ceremony of the Olympics…if dancing, drinking, and liposuction were among the events.

We fed off the crowd's energy, spinning and bouncing randomly through the linear parade stadium. Any technical dancing was impossible with these costumes, which was probably the general idea. The judges might have knocked off a few points if we hadn't been weighed down and camouflaged with feathers.

The nearest *director de harmonia* kept yelling at us (this is what *directors de harmonia* do) to stay in neat rows, sing louder, show more enthusiasm and look happier. We couldn't have been any happier, at least not without medication. Or maybe that's what the director was suggesting.

It takes twenty-five minutes to dance through the Sambodromo. And at the end, exhausted, my neck muscles cramping, my cheeks stuck in perma-grin, I took my $250 costume (which would never survive the plane ride home) and, like most of the other participants, dumped it right in the trash.

It was an absolutely fantastic, unforgettable experience. Now if you'll excuse me, I have to get back to scrubbing my feet.

Kiss a Gift Horse in the Mouth

In the Middle of Italy's Palio

SIENA, ITALY

THE PALIO, STARTED IN 1597, IS AN ABSOLUTELY fantastic, universally appreciated annual horse race. That is unless you happen to be one of the horses that crash into the stone embankments as racers careen around the medieval city plaza; one of the jockeys who get bucked off or beaten up by locals for throwing the race; or among the thousands of spectators who have trouble coping with 100-degree temperatures during the four-day event while standing in the packed viewing area next to elderly German tourists with big hair and unusual personal body fragrances. Otherwise, like I said, it's fantastic.

The Palio is held twice a year—July 2 and August 16—but the real start of these two events takes place three days before each race.

On the morning of August 13, I wound my way through the twisting Tuscan town of Siena to the striking Piazza del Campo, a D-shaped cobblestone plaza framed by five-story apartment buildings along the curve and a city hall with a fifteen-story bell tower along the straight-away. The outer ring of the Campo was covered with clay, making a 300-yard-long D-shaped track. Cafés along the curve had set up bleachers in front of their entrances for viewing and charged a small fortune (between $25 and $50) for people to sit and watch each practice. Like most of the crowd, I looked on for free from the infield.

About forty-eight thoroughbreds were given trial runs in six separate heats so everyone could get an idea of how each horse handled the corners. I witnessed about five accidents in which corner-challenged steeds either overran the turn and smashed into the wall (one of which was lined with queen-size mattresses for this very reason) or cut the corner too close, hit the inside post, catapulted the rider into the crowd, and limped off the track. In the end, ten horses not in traction were selected for the Palio.

At noon, representatives of the seventeen *contrade* (competing neighborhoods in Siena, each with a mascot and its own racing colors) attended the *tratta,* a bingolike drawing to decide which *contrada* would get which horse. Everyone seemed able to discern the favored horse from the *brenna* (el sucko). So when the folks from each *contrada* learned which horse they had drawn, they either screamed and danced down the street singing the praise of their first-round draft pick or ran off wailing and exhibiting the sort of emotion normally reserved for Lars von Trier movies.

For the next two days, the horses ran two practice heats per day, at 9 A.M. and 7 P.M., with the crowds growing progressively bigger at each race. The more muscular members of rival *contrade*, such as the "Ducks" and the "Towers," would get into spectacular brawls after each practice run. The fights lasted about five minutes before the police would separate them by ten yards, at which distance they would chant Palio songs at each other, each group trying to be louder and, apparently, more out of tune than the other.

The jockeys, wearing the colors of the *contrade* they were paid to represent, dressed for each practice race as though they were heading off to a Renaissance-era pajama party. Some jockeys let their horses go fast and get used to the course, while others wanted their steeds to conserve energy and not risk injury. It was hard to tell how much of this was left to the discretion of the jockeys, all of whom apparently came from Sardinia and rode (always bareback, by Palio regulation) for whichever *contrada* paid them the most money.

My favorite aspect of the event was the *mortaretto* (cannon), which fired a brain-shaking blast that scared the tortellini out of me the first few times I heard it. It was fired to let people know the horses were entering the *campo*, when the first horse crossed the finish line after three laps, and a few times for no apparent reason. After I got used to it, I took great pleasure in watching Palio neophytes, including corpulent businessmen, spill their drinks, shriek in fear, or crap themselves when it reverberated through the piazza.

On Friday evening after the practice run I went to what I first thought was the Palio Carnevale. It had the usual assortment of kiddy rides and music performances, but was completely arranged, I learned, by the Communist party, who were giving speeches on the main stage throughout the event. While nearly all the booths inside the carnival grounds were selling knick-knacks, cell phones, security systems, even Culligan watercoolers. No one seemed to notice that the Communist party was being financed by ambitious capitalists.

On Saturday, the night before the big race, each *contrada* hosted a pep-rally dinner. I paid $30 for a plate with $10 worth of food and the privilege of eating with 700 members of the Aquila *contrada* (mascot: two-headed eagle). Hopefully the money went toward something useful, like paying off another jockey to throw the race or designing a less mutated-looking mascot. The meal stopped several times for singing. Fortunately, many of the songs were easy to follow because the only word in the entire song was the horse's name, which in our case was Votta Votta. Perhaps the horse had a stutter.

Each *contrada's* horse is deified, and if you think I'm kidding, just watch (on Siena's local TV channel) the horses brought inside the church to get blessed by a priest. Moreover, the steeds don't live in stables but closely guarded "horse houses" that are reportedly cleaner and better kept than any single home in Siena. *Contrade* members spoonfeed the horses, touch them for good luck, and—I actually saw some men do this—kiss them on the lips. I doubt there's any tongue involved, but I wouldn't rule it out completely.

To view the actual race, you must either pony up several hundred dollars for one of the few bleacher seats not reserved for the *contrade* or arrive at the infield early— around 8 A.M. for a standing position along the rail or by 3 P.M. for a decent spot in the center. At 5 P.M. the infield resembles the front-row crush of a Boyzone concert. No one under six feet can see much, and the sun is melting you like a triple scoop of gelato in a convection oven. Actually, most of us would have gladly exchanged several vital organs for even a spoonful of gelato. It was a giant sweatfest.

The Palio procession begins at 6 P.M. with a pair of flag bearers in medieval costume from each *contrada* performing a five-minute routine of flag waving at several points around the *campo*. The crowd was thrilled with the first pair and amused by the second and third, but by the time the tenth pair completed their fourth routine an hour later, the flag waving had lost its charm and most of the people around me had wedged themselves to the ground to read a book.

This impressive display was followed by an ox-drawn cart displaying the Palio. Until this moment, I had no idea that the Palio was anything other than the name of this event. It turns out it's a seven-foot-tall painted silk banner with a new design created each year—the trophy for the winning *contrada*. I wouldn't even dream of making any derogatory remarks about this historical award—it was clearly a work of art, although this year's design looked about as moving as a Hello Kitty poster.

With a blast of the *mortaretto,* the horses entered the *campo,* with each jockey selecting a stick from a batch proffered by a police officer. The sticks were not only for whipping the horses, but for slashing the other jockeys—a highly encouraged aspect of the race, although it can't begin until the race is underway. Which wasn't as soon as we had hoped.

The Palio *mossa* (start) is a sordid and often drawn-out affair. All the horses must enter a holding pen set up between two *canape* (large ropes) before they are allowed to start. And they must be arranged in a certain order determined by a last-minute lottery. Once the *rincorsa* (tenth horse) has entered the pen, the front *canapa* drops and the riders are off. Sounds simple enough.

However, the *rincorsa* jockey doesn't want to enter the pen until the rest of the horses are in disarray. So he just waits, and waits, and the anxious (and, most likely, pharmaceutically charged) horses take care of the rest. The timing has to be just right, because if the rambunctious horses get too out of order, the starter tells them to all go back out and try again. This happened several times, each time with a collective moan from the tens of thousands packed into the *campo,* as a few hundred more collapsed from heatstroke.

After at least thirty minutes of jumbled starts, the horses were off, sprinting along the arching curve of the D-shaped course. As they entered the first sharp turn, connecting the curve and the straightaway, three horses went down, slamming into the mattresses along the wall like downhill skiers hitting the safety net—only you have to imagine a safety net with a stone wall directly behind it. One horse struggled back up and sped off after the pack sans jockey, another got up limping with a visibly broken, dangling leg, and the third horse never got back up at all.

Members from the *contrade* of the injured horses ran heartbroken and weeping to the aid of their thoroughbreds. Anxious to prevent their horses from becoming a spectacle, the more muscular members kept a lookout, ready to beat up and rip the film away from any amateur photographer who tried to preserve the moment.

Meanwhile the rest of the pack continued galloping around the course. On the second lap the lead jockey fell off his horse (possible bribe?), but his mount continued in the lead. Under the Palio's rules, it would be allowed to win without its jockey. However, on the final stretch, it was passed by the Wave's horse (and jockey), prompting the Wave *contrada* to go absolutely nuts. They stormed the track, grabbed the Palio banner, and marched their horse through town and into the cathedral for a semireligious festivity that filtered back into the streets and continued until morning.

Some say the Palio is cruel to horses and plagued with cheating. Which is true. Many Italians (mostly from outside Siena) want the race banned. Others have proposed—quite reasonably, I think—that they replace the thoroughbreds with stock horses, which are less likely to crash and more likely to recover if they do.

So far, the opposition has only managed to institute a horse nursing home for the crippled victims of former races. On this issue, I had a few locals point out that most animals that come into contact with humans meet a much crueler fate, whether it's a sickly gold fish that gets the flush, a rat that tests cosmetics, an elephant locked inside a tiny zoo cage, or the public humiliation that some pet owners inflict when they dress up their dogs in little matching outfits.

The biggest danger of the Palio, however, is to humans. A few of the police I spoke with were concerned about a potential stampede. Not by the horses, but by the 40,000-plus spectators, should a panic arise in the exit-limited *campo*. Danger is clearly part of the Palio's tradition, so they suggest that those who find it too unsettling should simply stay away.

One of the less obvious aspects of the Palio that deserves note is the absence of advertising. Local government officials, much to their credit, have resisted the generous offers to plaster the *campo* with giant promotions for companies like Coke, Fuji Film, or—God forbid—Elmer's Glue.

PART FIVE

FREESTYLE EMPLOYMENT

The Grateful Med

Working a Month at Club Med in Bali

BALI, INDONESIA

"LIFE AS IT SHOULD BE" IS WHAT CLUB MED'S BROCHURE says. But there's so much hype surrounding this international chain of resorts it's hard to know what to really think. Some facilities cater to families, some cater to couples, but the prevailing reputation is that Club Med is to hedonists what *Romper Room* is to five year olds—a utopian sanctuary where sports like coed naked Twister are actually played, and you get free liposuction if you can't fit into your Speedo.

The Club Med in Bali (a mix of families, couples, and singles) was covered with blindingly green grass and manicured gardens in full bloom and bordered by a sprawling white beach on one side and a golf course on the other; if this wasn't paradise, it was close. I guessed there wouldn't be a large selection of jobs available, so I prepared myself for the worst when I rode up on my rented moped for an unscheduled meeting with the manager, the so-called *chef du village.*

Chef du village: "Can you be zee anstructor uv arrowbicks?"

Me: "It's been a while since I last taught aerobics. If possible, I'd prefer something else." (Translation: My aerobics experience entails one class in which I was the token male in the back of the room, completely out of sync with everyone else.)

Chef du village: "Wee also need ah dis jokey. Can you do zis?"

Me: "Sure. I'm familiar with audio electronics." (Translation: But I can't manage anything more complex than a Walkman.)

I was hired to work as a DJ au pair G.O. The "G.O." part stood for *gentil organisateur,* Club Med's version of the camp counselor. "Au pair" meant they wouldn't pay me anything, but I'd get a free room, excellent food, and full use of the facilities when not working. It also meant I didn't have to sign the standard six-month contract, so I could leave at will without repercussions.

I got my DJ training from an Australian who was planning to leave. He supervised me while I learned the complex workings of the strobe light (push the red button) and the disco ball (push the white button) and looking cool (hold the DJ headphones so they cover only one ear). The problem was that I didn't recognize the names on more than a few albums, since I generally don't buy dance music —I just listen to it when I'm out dancing. The Australian put all the current hits into one box so I couldn't go wrong.

My other task was making sure the guests were happy.

I worked with a French improvisational actor on the "Animation Team." We were like police on Prozac, an international task force of happiness. We'd meet in the costume room at 10:15 A.M. and again at 2:30 P.M. to put on some goofball outfit. (We had a massive wardrobe at our disposal and a full-time costume maker!) Then we'd go out and accost the guests with dumb pranks for half an hour.

In the first two weeks, I dressed up as Rambo, Indiana Jones, Wonder Woman, a baby, a caveman, a French cook, a prerevolutionary French princess, part of a Chinese New Year dragon, a musketeer, a ballerina, a French nurse, a mummy...you get the idea.[1]

It was amazing what we could get away with—things that just wouldn't fly in the real world. We'd walk around the pool and throw in anyone who looked grumpy. Other times we'd dress up as doctors and smear red makeup on the unsuspecting faces of guests we "examined" on the golf course. We'd dress as cavemen and run around thumping the bottoms of sunbathing guests with our styrofoam clubs. As bizarre as it sounds, this was what we were *supposed* to do—and, apparently, the guests were enjoying it. For about two hundred bucks a day, they'd better.

I got the feeling that each Club Med is like a little embassy, and not just because of its international staff and guests. Club Med's policies on nudity, drinking, and sexual promiscuity can be substantially different from the countries they're located in. There seems to be a quid pro quo with the local governments. Club Med pays their taxes and hires locals to clean the rooms and mow the lawn. In return, Club Med is granted "diplomatic immunity."

Needless to say, Club Med's drinking policy was pretty loose. In fact, we were *encouraged* to drink on the job. The chef du village even provided us with a monthly allotment of "bar beads," the unique Club Med monetary system

---

[1] The idea being that I should try to get a refund for my college education.

where four white plastic beads equal one orange bead, two orange equal one yellow, and four yellows mean that you won't realize you just spent $8 for a shot glass-sized beer.

After a few days, I was convinced I had found the best job on the planet. But by the fourth week, the routine was beginning to wear on me. After doing the traditional Club Med line dances, say, fifty times, they began to feel as dopey as they looked. Even secretly painting the toenails of the guests from under the buffet table while they put food on their plates (my favorite prank) got old.

Conversation with my surrogate family of G.O.s never got any deeper than a Club Med brochure. Discussing current events simply wasn't appropriate in a place that wouldn't be affected by anything short of an all-out nuclear war. The G.O.s were a very accepting group, but I attributed this to the fact that most seemed to be escaping something, from an old relationship to the rat race. Club Med, it seems, is like the French Foreign Legion for the pacifist with social skills.

I'm still convinced this is one of the best gigs on the planet—in the right-sized doses. Like eating ice cream sundaes: the first and second ones taste great, the third is still pretty good, but after number twelve, your stomach hurts, you realize you have no substance in your diet, and you've gained five pounds.

It was difficult to bring myself to quit at the end of my fifth week. The food was still outstanding, the "village" still felt like it had been cut out of a brochure, and my biggest decision was still whether to go windsurfing, sea kayaking, or golfing after lunch. But when I began to feel trapped in the Biosphere of Happiness I had helped create for the guests to escape civilization, like a prisoner of utopian life who had run out of Chapstick for his perma-smile, I knew it was time to move on.

Underwater Bellhopping

Carrying Bags to the Underwater Hotel

KEY LARGO, FLORIDA

I'M TWENTY FEET UNDERWATER RIGHT NOW. BEEN HERE all night. Even fell asleep for eight hours. Fortunately, there's an entire ventilated hotel down here.

To get to my room, I had to scuba dive. There's no other way in. Or out. I swear I'm not making any of this up.

I had read a small blurb about Jules' Undersea Lodge in some inflight magazine, but I didn't quite believe it. If it was real, I remember thinking, how do they get luggage to the rooms?

When I called up, Ron, the hotel manager, told me they get "the luggage question" all the time.[1] To get to the bottom of this (literally), I made arrangements to work for a day as an underwater bellboy, and then to spend the night.

Jules' Undersea Lodge, originally dubbed La Chalupa, was originally used as an underwater research laboratory off

---

[1] The second most common question is if guests can bring their pets along. Ron's answer: only goldfish.

the coast of Puerto Rico. In 1986 it was moved to Key Largo and converted into a hotel. Roughly 7,000 overnight guests have swum through since then. According to Ron, they've all lived to tell about it.

Now about the baggage. First, you load the suitcases on a mini-submarine and drive down to the hotel. No, actually, you drop the gear into a trash bag, throw a few rocks in, and let it sink. No, that's not true either. My point is, the whole idea of an underwater hotel is so wacky, just about any luggage delivery system would seem plausible in context.

The head bellboy (also "mer-chef," head of housekeeping, and concierge), Mike Smith, didn't have much difficulty making the shift from the U.S. Navy to an underwater hotel. He looks a bit like Rod Stewart with a beer gut, and years in the engine room have left him with a booming voice.

Mike taught me how to bring the luggage down without ("keep your fingers crossed") getting anything wet. The way it actually works—I am now telling the truth—is that you divide up your belongings into small, washload-size portions, then let Mike wrap them in plastic bags (one plastic bag for clothes, two bags for computers and cameras), place them in water-resistant plastic suitcases, attach lead weights, and swim them down from the departure dock.

My first luggage run was just a little tricky. The suitcase is easy to swim with, but once you arrive at the barnacle-covered hotel—or, rather, at the entrance hole underneath it—getting the weighted case up out of the water takes some doing. You have to swim under the ballast, plant your feet on the bottom, and military press it up over your head. With the case finally up, I poked my head through the Jacuzzi-size hole and pulled off my mask. I was now halfway inside the lobby.

Some natural reflex made me hesitant to take my first breath. When I finally did inhale, the air tasted about the same as the dry, compressed air I was breathing through my regulator. There's no chandelier or winding staircase in the lobby, which is about the size of a walk-in closet. At the far end of the room, there's a shower with an unlimited supply of water and a foot-pump-action toilet.

There was no time to explore the rest of the hotel—I had work to do. Or so I thought. After about five or six runs, Mike told me that I was done. The hotel was filled to capacity, but that only meant four people: Mary, a twenty-five-year-old waitress from Virginia; Brian, fireman her boyfriend; Signe; and me. A good portion of the luggage I had bellhopped was my own. Thus, the tip situation basically took care of itself.

I peeled out of my wetsuit, took a hot shower, and changed into jeans and a t-shirt. The others were way ahead of me and had already begun socializing in the living/dining room. Mary, a diving enthusiast, was explaining how she had dragged Brian along to fulfill her dream of living beneath the sea.

From above, the hotel looks like a pair of binoculars. There are two horizontal cylinders connected by a rectangular middle part, which is the Jacuzzi-like entrance room/lobby. In one cylinder, you've got a kitchenette with two small, mermaid-motif dining tables, ceiling-to-floor carpeting, a TV, and one porthole window. The other cylinder is divided into two small living quarters, each with bunk beds, a TV, and a porthole window. The quarters are about as tight as you would expect on a private yacht…or a sunken one.

According to Ron, some nut (my word, not his) stayed down here for sixty-nine days just to prove it could be done. He may have been cut off from daylight, but not from the rest of the world. There's a regular phone line, a Navy-style phone, a CB radio, and an intercom—better communications than any sealed habitat on the planet except maybe Air Force One.

To get from the lobby to the rooms or dining area, you need to pass through a narrow, round opening—the kind that connects modules in space stations. Which makes sense, considering that the hotel has been used as a study facility for NASA. And it may explain why the staff doesn't say you're staying at the hotel; they call you an "aquanaut" and say you're "on a mission."

And a pricey mission it is: $325 per person with an early check-in and late check-out (called the "Luxury Aquanaut Package"). It's hard to throw this much money into the water without owning a boat.

What do you do down here? Watch videos, mostly. There are plenty to chose from: *Hunt for Red October, Splash, Cocoon, The Abyss, 20,000 Leagues under the Sea.* Even *Waterworld.* The only thing I couldn't find is the Beatles' *Yellow Submarine*—but then again I didn't quite have the energy to search for it. (The pumped-in air we were breathing contained a relaxing 10 percent more oxygen than surface air, so after an hour of watching videos, we were all itching to take a nap. This was fine, since we had no desire to be active, but it might prove awkward for the honeymooners who pay $1,000 a night to get the place to themselves.)

You can also gaze out the forty-two-inch windows, but the visibility is piss poor. The hotel isn't situated in transparent waters off the coast with schools of colorful fish swimming by, but in the tiny, murky "emerald lagoon."

Looking out the windows has the effect of peering into a fish tank in need of a few more of those sucker fish that eat up algae. The few fish I did see out the window seemed to be more interested in looking at us in our human tank.

If you're feeling motivated, you can take the underwater version of a stroll in the lagoon. The overnight price includes unlimited access to tank-free diving from the hotel with long "hookah" tubes. They've sprinkled the bottom of the lagoon with some archaeological artifacts and a few fake silver bars for your diving pleasure. The only problem, again, is that the visibility sucks. The best part for me was simply going in and out of the hotel. Imagine waving good-bye to your friends and disappearing with a jump into the Jacuzzi. An exit worthy of Hugh Hefner.

Around 6 P.M., mer-chef Mike arrived with a bellowing "hello" and dinner. I had ordered a lobster tail, but once it was on my plate, I felt a bit uncomfortable eating it—like dining on a steak in a cow pasture.

I found the food entirely enjoyable, but those who are expecting the advertised "gourmet meals" may find it comes up a tad short. Unless granola bars and chips count as gourmet appetizers and a gourmet breakfast means taking your own frozen waffles out of the fridge and warming them in the microwave.

What you're left with is pondering how cool it is to be staying underwater. Which is exactly what we did while we watched videos. And I must admit, watching *The Abyss* underwater gives it a whole new feeling: horror film.

If you'll excuse me, I need to get some air.

Oh My Guinness

Taste-Testing and Making Brew in Dublin

DUBLIN, IRELAND

THIS IS GUINNESS COUNTRY. I'M TALKING ABOUT THE beer that looks like discarded brake fluid with a bubble bath-foam head. It's the best beer in the world if you ask the people here in Dublin. Some even say it's in their blood. And with the amount I've seen people drinking, I don't doubt it for a minute.

To confirm such wild claims, I went straight to the Guinness brewery. To work, of course. Mostly as a professional taste-tester.

I don't know what sort of pictures pop into your head when you try to imagine what the Guinness brewery might be like. Maybe little green men dancing around black kettles of fermenting barley; red-haired Lavernes and Shirleys capping bottled brew with shamrock-green rubber gloves; or beer-guzzling giants who look like they're about to give birth to quadruplets milling around with their pants conspicuously low on the waist.

Whatever the case may have been in 1759 when Arthur

Guinness purchased Mark Rainsford's ale brewery to begin producing his own recipe, I can report that it is now a state-of-the-art rig churning out about 1,000,000,000 mugs of beer annually. Or, as the people at Guinness like to say, 4.6 million hectoliters. The people at Guinness are always speaking in "hectoliters." I have no idea what amount they could possibly be referring to, but I usually nod my head, hoping to assure them that America hasn't sent over a journalist who doesn't know what the hecto they're talking about.

As James Joyce wrote in *Ulysses,* "A puzzle would be to cross Dublin without passing a pub." These days, a tougher puzzle would be to cross Dublin without passing a Guinness promotion. Guinness's presence is as prominent as Fran Drescher's accident, placing the company firmly in the soul of the Irish.[1]

My first task was making some beer[2] in the brew house with third-generation Guinness man and brewery manager, Shay Doyle and in the fermenting plant (called the FBP, which, as far as I was concerned, stood for "Free Beer Place") with third-generation Guinness beer tester Donal Prior.

When I say I made the beer, what I mean is that I pushed a couple of buttons at the two NASA-like beer-control centers that mixed in the barley, hops, and yeast and

---

[1] However, after touring the plant, I liked to joke with some of the guys that Guinness was more international than the management might care to admit. "How so?" they'd ask. Well, the hops came from Oregon, New Zealand and Australia, there are Scottish holding tanks, German electronic systems, and, as of six months ago, English financial control. Needless to say, no one found this "joke" very funny.

[2] Don't worry, it was just for the German market.

cleaned the tanks—at least that's what I thought I was doing. All I saw were some blinking letters on the computer screen as the beer, hops, yeast, and cleaning agents ran though some twenty miles of pipes—a maze of metal tubing in the next room that made me feel like I was walking around inside a giant microchip.

With a few keystrokes, I accomplished in a few minutes what used to take about 1,000 men a full day to complete. In the '70s, this traditional, family-run brewery employed 4,000 people. Today there are just 400 full-time employees, and the brewery is making 30 percent more beer (though I'm not sure if that's because Guinness is producing more beer or the employees are drinking less). Before automation, there was a "decent population" of workers called "swampers" who drank upwards of three gallons a day, and I heard rumors of a few heavyweights who could drain six gallons!

Back then, all employees got vouchers for two pints a day to drink on site, and they were offered more as incentive. Today, drinking on the job (except tasting) is forbidden, but all employees can bring home four cases every three months, which, according to brewing shift manager Chris Molamphy, makes them pretty popular on the BBQ circuit.

Next came the taste-testing. There's a lot more to Guinness than meets the palate. According to Fergal Murray, the "sensory manager," the foam has to be within millimeters of the correct height: half an inch. The smell, color, and carbonation are all vital, and each batch of beer is carefully tested before it leaves the premises. Testing it might sound like a dream job. But here's a little taste of reality that might change your view: The brewery is in operation twenty-four hours a day, which means the fresh brews aren't just tested after work with a bowl of peanuts and a game of rugby. They need to be tested at 6 A.M. and 8 A.M. as well. I enjoy the beer, but I can't say I'd be eager to slide one back at the crack of dawn with a bowl of cornflakes, followed by a chaser two hours later.

Some say the Guinness in Dublin tastes better, or at least different. And, in most cases, they'd be right. To cater to the 150 Guinness-importing countries, Guinness makes seventeen slightly different blends under the same label—all with airport-baggage-like codes.

For the German market, they make a 5 percent brew called Draft Stout, or DS. Africa gets a 7 percent alcohol batch (Foreign Extra Stout, or FES). And Belgians, accustomed to serious alcohol content, get a highly aromatic 8 percent edition (Guinness X-port Stout, or GXS). The Guinness made for the Irish market has 4.3 percent alcohol (called Irish Draft Stout, or IDS) and is exactly the same as the beer that Guinness ships to the U.S. But it took me several painstaking testing sessions to learn to distinguish the difference between all these brews—not to mention the difference between draft, bottled, and canned beer—without slurring my words,. And I'd be happy to share the findings of my extended testing if I could recall any of it.

The Guinness taste may take some getting used to. But as they say, once you go Guinness, there's no going back. Possibly because you can't remember how to get there.

Surfing by a Thread

Sewing Shorts at Patagonia, Inc.

VENTURA, CALIFORNIA

PART OF TRAVELING IS LEARNING GEOGRAPHY, AND AT the moment most of America is under the impression that the land of Patagonia is located somewhere on the front of a fleece jacket. Of course, this is not true. It's located on polypropylene long underwear.

I didn't go to work at Patagonia, the California-based outdoor gear manufacturer, in the traditional sense: getting paid to do something useful. I was just allowed—thanks to Steve the Media Relations Director—to make the world's most amazing pair of travel shorts and stay in Patagonia's beach-front guest house (this after Steve found out I was planning to camp in my car in his parking lot).

It's very important that I have items like the world's most amazing pair of travel shorts because when I travel I only have room in my small pack to bring one of everything. (Yes, even underwear.)

There are two schools of thought when it comes to dressing on the road: (1) stay in the same town and change your clothes every day; and (2) wear the same clothes and change locations. In the end, with a lot of deodorant, both have the same effect.

The first order of business was to figure out a blueprint, so I went and had a chat with Piers, a designer in the Sailing, Fishing, and Surfing Division. I sat down in Piers's office, which contained a desk and two bean-bag chairs on the floor behind it, and we discussed my options. I wanted to put together an extremely high-tech pair of shorts with a lot of bells and whistles (actually zippers and Velcro) that I had designed on a napkin. Piers looked at my design and told me it would take a month to accomplish since we both knew I was barely qualified to make a sock. Piers and Steve ended up deciding that a "simple" pair of Baggies shorts would be challenging enough, even though I volunteered to stay in Patagonia's guest house for a year if necessary.

The next step was to cut the fabric. But Sam the Fabric Cutter was busy, so Steve, Piers, and I went surfing. Right in the middle of the day! Patagonia is only a five-minute dash from the beach, so, not surprisingly, we ran into several other employees out there. What does Patagonia's founder and president, Yvon Chouinard, think about this? His philosophy is "When the waves are good, we surf. When they're bad, we work." Corporate America has much to learn from this man.

The main problem with my little shorts-making adventure was that I can't sew to save my life. The last time I turned on a sewing machine I ended up in the hospital. Really. I was attempting to stitch a hand-puppet in my eighth-grade home economics class when I accidentally sewed over a pin, which broke the sewing machine needle and sent a shard of it into my left eyeball. I was rushed to the hospital and they put this special contraption on my eye to keep me from blinking. Then they doused my eye with, I think, shampoo. Or it felt that way. Finally, the doctor walked in and pulled the shard out with a tweezers. But I digress.

Under the watchful eyes of Barbara and Gloria, professional seamstresses in Patagonia's prototype construction area, I practiced stitching lines across scraps of cloth, making sure there wasn't a stray pin within three miles of my sewing machine. These machines are the stock cars of the sewing world—0 to 600 stitches in one second. My biggest problem was threading them, which took me around thirty minutes. And that was with the "easy" machines. Some machines, such as the dreaded "mulitstitch," take Barbara—who can thread a needle in the dark—forty-five minutes to set up.

Barbara was determined to make each of my stitches as good as hers, which, I tried to explain, was simply not possible. I would sew something that looked fine to me, but Barbara (who was otherwise very nice) would take it from me, remove the stitches, and have me do it again. It was a slight battle of wills: I just wanted something that would hold together; she wanted stitches straight enough to calibrate scientific instruments.

Gloria, on the other hand, was a bit more laid back with my work. She only took exception to my major goofs, like when I accidentally made a hole the size of a police badge in the fabric and then when I sewed an overlap that gave the shorts slots for someone with four legs.

My Baggies mandated the use of nearly every machine in the place, including the buttonhole maker, which was my favorite. You just put the material in place, stomp on the pedal, and—THWUNK—there's your buttonhole. If I ever settle down, I'm definitely going to get one of these babies for home use. I can't tell you right now what I'd do use it for, but I'm sure I'll find a full range of things that need buttonholes.

By the third day, I was familiar enough with the machines that when Barbara would say, "Doug, you need the double-stitch overlock machine," I knew to get up and ask Steve if we could go surfing.

Barbara tried to explain the importance of what I was doing. The environmental idea is that you are not just making these shorts for yourself. If you make them well, she said they'd last long enough that several people could use them. That's just one of the interesting philosophies of this company. Mr. Chouinard, who encourages environmental activism and gives paid maternity and paternity leave, likes to hire "dirt bags"— outdoors enthusiasts who have taken out a second mortgage on their home so they can buy even more of Patagonia's products. Mr. Chouinard believes that (if I may paraphrase) it's easier to teach an outdoorsy person to work a copying machine than teach a business person how to crap in the woods.

After three quick days I had finished the shorts, which were black with orange thread and looked remarkably like a pair of Doc Martens shoes. I brought them over to Mr. Chouinard for inspection. Yvon, not a tall man, was wearing a soiled t-shirt and flip-flops and working on Patagonia's new surfboard line when I caught up with him. He held my XXL shorts up to his waist; the bottoms nearly came down to his ankles.

He smiled. "Looks like you teamed up with Omar the Tent Maker," he said.

Then Steve and Piers came along and I put my shorts through the rigorous ditch-work-and-go-surfing test—a key element of Patagonia's product development. I didn't set any trends on the waves, but that may have been because no one managed to see my shorts in the microsecond I was actually standing up on the board.

Behind the Baggage Carousel

Working at Heathrow Airport

LONDON, ENGLAND

IF YOU'VE EVER BEEN TO AN INTERNATIONAL AIRPORT, then you're already familiar with concourses that seem to stretch half the distance to the place you're flying to, vacuum-packed $7 sandwiches with lettuce the consistency of wet toilet paper, and the practice of waiting for connecting flights that have the same chance of departing on time as a French rock group producing a Top 40 hit.

What you're probably less familiar with is the underworld of services that buttress air travel. To get a closer look, I went behind the scenes at London's Heathrow Airport.

When Heathrow opened on January 1, 1946, with a flight to Buenos Aires, few imagined it would go on to become the world's largest waiting lounge. Or airport. It now boasts the most international flights, and over 60 million travelers traipse through it each year, some of them still in possession of their own luggage.

I was able to arrange much of this experience thanks to the terribly kind British Airways media person, Lisa

Preston, who, by airport public relations law, had to accompany me at all times to keep me from wandering astray. I was thankful for this. Because if you think the inside of Heathrow makes for difficult navigation, you need to be born and raised on the premises to grasp the exterior, a chaotic land of little luggage trucks, fuel trucks, catering trucks, emergency vehicles, buses, shuttles, all fitted with orange blinking lights and following a traffic system comprised of little yellow lines seemingly painted on the tarmac by an assistant producer from TV's *Bloopers and Practical Jokes*.

My first physical exercise occurred at Terminal One, where I joined up with the baggage handlers to try my hand at peeking at passengers' undergarments—or whatever it is they do there. Actually, I made a comment along these lines to my baggage-handling escorts (two frighteningly muscular union representatives who could easily crush me like a Diet Coke can) but, fortunately, they didn't notice: working beside airplane engines had rendered them nearly deaf. They wouldn't have appreciated it much because the Terminal One baggage staff had, I later learned, picked up a dodgy reputation years ago for occasional lapses in judgment. They didn't feel like furnishing any of the details when I rephrased the question, but I am happy to pass along their firm assurances that whatever was happening before is absolutely not happening any longer.

After changing into a white jumpsuit with a fluorescent yellow vest, which made me look like those space dweebs that dance around in the Pentium processor commercials, I was able to join my escorts (who did not particularly care to be mentioned in this story) for baggage removal of an inbound flight from Oslo. The best part of the job—something

I'd always wanted to do—was riding up the little luggage conveyor belt into the hold of the plane. They wouldn't let me surf it standing up, so I ascended backward on my tail end, and that was just fine.

Hunched over in the five-foot-high, ventilation-free compartment in the belly of the plane, it took about five minutes to toss—I mean "transfer"—the bags onto the conveyor. The more time-consuming part was handling the additional cargo—heavy, sealed buckets of "biological hazard." My escorts said this substance is no problem unless it spills. In which case, they call in a special biodisposal team. Comforting.

With the plane emptied, I figured we'd drive the now-filled little luggage train over to the carousel pickup area, where we would let it sit for forty-five minutes before actually putting it on the carousel. But this was not possible because the people who drive the little luggage train have their own union (Union of Cute Luggage Transports), and Lisa hadn't cleared my visit with them. So we returned to the dispatch center, where, between flights, the baggage-handling men (no women had worked in this capacity since the airport opened in 1946) play pool and read the paper in little segregated groups according to which soccer team they support.

However, if I've led you to believe moving luggage is a labor of leisure, I should elucidate: these guys are out there in all weather extremes, at ridiculous times of night, risking hernia and hearing to get you your eighty-pound duffel bag holding at least three outfits you'll never wear. From what I witnessed, I'm surprised they don't lose more luggage. In just twenty minutes on the tarmac, I managed to lose my notepad.

Today Heathrow can boast (the airport's PR office actually does boast this in a news release called "Fun Facts") daily recovery of twenty lost mobile phones, the recovery of the front end of a Ford Escort, a glass eye, and a lost suitcase of dead fish.

Which should be a nice lead-in to the next topic: airline food.

Airline food has been given a bad rap for decades, and I don't want to scare anyone further when I say that I helped prepare some of the in-flight meals. Not to worry: I was wearing plastic gloves, a lab jacket, and a rather unflattering hair net, and I managed to refrain from scratching myself most of the time. So if you find fault with your next meal, I can assure you it was made by a different travel writer.

Gate Gourmet handles the in-flight cuisine for British Airways and produces tens of thousands of meals per day—all of it made the same day or the day before, depending on when the flight leaves. The lobster served in first class was being individually prepared by a lone chef. The economy-class meal was put together assembly style by a team of five. I jumped in for a while, then quickly jumped back out as I fell behind the pace of the women in front of me and mucked up their rhythm.

It was nearing noon so we (Lisa Preston and I) opted for a meal: a business-class lunch. It was delicious—much tastier than anything I remember eating on board a plane. Gate Gourmet says that this is because our palates change with the altitude and the scented cabin air; we lose roughly a quarter of our taste sensitivity. Although this doesn't explain why peanuts taste better.

I switched chaperones for my next task, clearing the runway, because Heathrow's management wanted their own PR person, the affable Emma Gaisford, to accompany me. Emma and I spent a few hours with the runway checkers, Tony and Patrick, who have, combined, served Heathrow for over fifty years. Their responsibility is to make sure the runways are clear of things like birds (which are strictly forbidden to use runways for taking off and landing) and "bits and pieces." That is to say, bits and pieces that have fallen off airplanes during take-off and landing. I'll bet you never realized there were bits and pieces dropping off airplanes to the degree that you needed an entire team of people to keep picking them up. Well, there are.

We didn't find any significant bits, such as an engine or wing, but there was a small chunk of tire. The best part was being so close to the planes during take-off and landing. To cover the nearly-three-kilometer-long runways without affecting the flow of traffic, we'd start at one end, facing the landing and departing planes and then, like a mismatched game of chicken, we'd charge at them, searching the runway for about thirty seconds before we'd have to make a quick exit onto the grass.

So, what sort of things do they find?

"Maybe a winglet[1] or blown-out tire," Tony explained. "Once I found a door from the underside of a plane. But we don't find that much stuff, and when we do, we can usually identify it and notify the airline. The smaller bits get blown off into the grass when planes take off and land," said Tony.

The real science is the bird chasing. More than ten species of birds live on and around the Heathrow airfield.

---

[1] A non-vital piece of the wing, from the way Tony made it sound. But I don't know for sure, and I didn't really want to ask.

From the air industry's standpoint, that's more than ten too many. Birds may have inspired flight, but now that we've got the hang of it, we don't want them around. A seagull sucked into the engine is seriously bad news. A duck can go through a pilot's windshield. The day before, in fact, a tiny starling had hit a plane's windshield. "But the windscreen was O.K.," Pat said.

"And the bird?" I asked.

"The bird was taken in for an autopsy," Tony said. I waited for the punchline, figuring the cause of death (head-on collision with jumbo jet) was pretty obvious.

But Tony continued, with a straight face, "They need to find out if the bird was eating something found on the airfield so we can get rid of it."

Airfield grass is maintained at eight inches, which has been scientifically proven to deter birds from feeding or settling. They even have a "Scarecrow machine," a device that simulates nine bird calls and is attached to large speakers mounted on the roof of a Range Rover. They can imitate aggressive birds to frighten off smaller ones, or simulate birds in heat to attract the males and lead them away Pied Piper style. For emergency situations, they have a flaregun with special "bird-scaring cartridges." Clearly this is serious business.

Saving what I thought would be the most fun for last (and it was), I was allowed to wash one of British Airways' Boeing 747 jumbo jets. It's a lot like washing a car, only B.A. has much better equipment, and I am specifically referring to the lift and sprayer, which gets you up about sixty feet in the air with a water gun strong enough to douse a fire or blow a protester down the street. I know this because I was hit with it. We were meant to be cleaning the plane, but I found it was much more fun to spray Paul, a B.A. plane cleaner on the other side of the jet. So we had a water fight over the top of the plane, and I didn't fare very well. Paul had the latest model. And my sprayer, although strong, by contrast gave a blast as powerful as an antiperspirant.

I finished the day soaked, with a newfound appreciation for the complexity of airport services I only used to complain about. By comparison, being a passenger is peanuts.

Sleeping on Thin Ice

Housekeeping at the Ice Hotel

JUKKASJÄRVI, SWEDEN

WHERE CAN YOU CHIP OFF A PIECE OF YOUR BED TO cool off your drink, deep-freeze a steak under your pillow while you sleep, or freeze your tongue to the wall of your hotel room should you try to lick it?

At the Ice Hotel, just north of the Arctic Circle.

So who, besides a Green Bay Packers fan, would be courageous enough (or brain damaged) to vacation in the wilds of northern Sweden in the middle of winter? Strangely enough, nearly everyone. Tourists from around the world are flocking to this giant ice cube. The Swedish Tourist Board, after years of searching, has finally found something to promote in the winter.

The hotel itself is an architectural marvel: 10,000 tons of snow and 5,000 tons of ice have been molded into an igloo big enough to sleep 100 guests or chill 400,000 12-packs of beer, depending on your personal preference. Built from scratch and redesigned every year, the hotel is now in its eighth season and is bigger and more elegant than ever. The only returning sculpture is the fiber optics–lit ice chandelier in the lobby, which also has a cozy ice lounge chair set in front of an ice fireplace with an ice moose head mounted over it, as well as a copy of an ice Bible on an ice bookshelf.

There's an ice cinema with ice seats (covered with reindeer skins) where you can watch films projected onto an ice wall, and even an ice church that hosts about forty weddings per year plus baptisms for babies with *is* (the Swedish word for "ice") in their names, such as Chris, Isabel, and Louise. I forgot to ask if English versions, like "Bernice," would qualify.

Then there's the Absolut Ice Bar. The bottle-shaped entryway is straight out of the famous Absolut ad campaign. Since all the bar glasses are made of ice ($3 per glass, overpriced alcohol not included), they don't serve scotch on the rocks, they serve scotch *in* the rocks!

The $80-per-night price tag was a little beyond my budget, so I defrayed some of the cost by working for several days as an "igloo guide." What does an igloo guide do? Hand out the sleeping bags, shake out the reindeer skins, give tours of the Ice Hotel, wake the guests in the morning, and clean up any yellow snow. In short, glorified housekeeping.

Unprepared for the minus-20-degree weather, like most guests, I borrowed some of the Ice Hotel's cold-weather gear. They give out snow suits and furry hats that would make Kate Moss look like Chewbaca.

What's it like to sleep in the Ice Hotel? Deathly quiet. The ice walls absorb all sound, which gives your room a slightly creepy feeling. The bed frames are made of ice, but have regular mattresses that are covered with reindeer skins for aesthetic effect. There's no room service to speak of and there are no phones, television, showers, ice, or toilets in the room. There's no popsicle waiting on your pillow before you go to bed and nothing is wrapped with little frozen doilies "for your protection." Basically, it's like a youth hostel that didn't pay its heating bill.

Just before it's time for bed, you swing by the reception and pick up a sleeping bag. When zipped properly, so that only your nose is sticking out of the bag's blow hole, it's plenty warm. You don't even notice the 25-degree air temperature. However, while sleeping, I must have unconsciously unzipped the bag. I woke up at 3 A.M. feeling like human sorbet.

The next morning in the men's sauna,[1] discussion of our sleeping experience in the ice hotel consisted mostly of who had to get up during the night and scamper through the ice lobby to the only toilet, located just outside the main door; who didn't have to go; who had to go more than once; who really had to go but held it, who tried to hold it but couldn't; who held it until the last possible moment, then had trouble with their sleeping-bag zippers and nearly wet themselves; and who never felt the urge to go because they (and one man actually seemed to be bragging about this) remembered to go right before they went to sleep!

Once I got the hang of things from my seven fellow igloo guides, the job was a snap. The only part I wasn't thrilled about was waking the guests in the morning with their complimentary cups of warm fruit drink. Some peo-

---

[1] A pre-breakfast sauna is included with the room charge, and nearly everyone takes advantage of it.

ple simply don't wake up until you're hovering over them and barking like a drill sergeant. And when they do finally bolt upright, you get an immediate whiff of morning breath—breath that could easily be classified as biohazard.

This duty was easily off-set by a few of the perks, such as acting as a judge for a corporate drink-mixing contest for the Absolut Vodka executives from Estonia. And, for the first time, I managed to get a good look at the northern lights, which is why many of the guests venture this far north. They were dazzling and entertaining (the northern lights, not the guests). But if I didn't know better, I would have thought that the wispy green celestial lights were not by Mother Nature's hand but toxic clouds drifting over from another meltdown in Russia.

Bum Deal

Ski Bumming the Hard Way in Val d'Isère

VAL D'ISÈRE, FRANCE

THERE'S NOTHING IN THE WORDS *SKI* OR *BUM* THAT implies any kind of work, which is exactly why I (and about a million other ski fanatics) find the concept so appealing. Imagine my surprise when, upon arriving in the French Alps for the winter season, I found out that the ski bums not only worked, but hardly had time to ski.

I spent my first week walking from ski shop to bakery to hotel to bar, begging for some kind of work in a language that didn't sound like French to anyone but me. At the beginning of the season in Val d'Isère, there were about 400 of us, mostly Europeans, competing for a handful of jobs, pacing the streets by day, then wandering into bars in the evenings and blowing $15 on beer to cleanse our souls.

I found some roommates who had discovered, by ski-bum standards, a great apartment—it was on the mountain and the toilets worked. Thanks to the town mayor, who held a real-estate monopoly, we had to pay the entire season's rent plus a security deposit in order to move in. That's a lot of money to put down if you don't have a job locked in or a grasp of the language. But I took the plunge. Even though I was sharing this studio apartment with four others (and sleeping in a triple-decker bunk bed), rent was still over $400 a month. It was ski-bum robbery, but there weren't any other options.

After making about eight rounds through the town's shops, an Italian named Paolo finally broke down and offered me a job as a waiter in his soon-to-be-opened Italian restaurant. It turned out to be an interesting experience—in much the same way that a trout might find it interesting to swim upstream, attempt to jump up a twenty-foot waterfall for two days, then land on a rock and die.

I was the first person hired. My restaurant experience included reluctantly clearing the table and rarely doing the dishes in my college apartment. That was just fine because Paolo's restaurant experience included driving a van with ski rental equipment for three years. Hard to believe, but compared to Paolo, I was overqualified.

After a few days Paolo hired two waitresses: Sylvie, a hyperactive thirty year old recently fired from a public relations firm in Paris, and Anna, an eighteen year old who was uncomfortable around people she didn't know. Neither had any restaurant experience. Marie, Paolo's wife, also had—SURPRISE!—no experience. Then Paolo hired Stephan, a stocky bartender with some experience. The problem was Stephan never spoke so we never got the benefit of his experience. Still, he was the veteran of the group, and we tried to respect that.

Everything was in place for a new sit-com series.

After a week of taking inventory, dusting the wall-mounted animal heads, and trying to get the cash register to open, the fat Italian cooks arrived. It was 11:30 A.M. and they had driven overnight from Milan. An hour later, a big shipment of food supplies arrived. And an hour after that the alcohol arrived. At 4:30 P.M., while I was helping stock the food, Paolo announced that we were going to open for dinner "tonight!"

I soon realized he was not joking and tried to convince him that this might not be a good idea: (1) we didn't have menus; (2) we didn't have enough plates; (3) we didn't have enough silverware; (4) we didn't have a fucking clue what we were supposed to do; (5) the previous restaurant's sign was still up; and (6) we had no way to communicate with the Italian cooks...just to name a few potential problems. Of course, none of these trivial details dissuaded Paolo.

Opening night, as even Nostradamus could have predicted, was a total disaster. Video footage of this evening would have been award-winning comedy material.

At about eight o'clock the first and only batch of customers came in. Marie took charge and seated each of the five groups in a different part of the restaurant. Sylvie decided to take responsibility for two tables on opposite ends of the restaurant. Anna, just as clueless, followed Sylvie's lead with her two tables. They were running back and forth the entire evening.

The menu problem had been solved simply enough. Sylvie made four of them with a blue crayon ten minutes before we opened. There were three choices of pasta written in Sylvie's Frenchlation of Italian. Our ordering system worked like this: The customer pointed to the meal on the menu, then we took the menu into the kitchen and pointed to the meal on the menu. The cooks tried to remember what we pointed to while they prepared the food.

Once the cooks got the food ready—this is my favorite part—they had to stand around holding the plates until we came in and took them because there was no place in the kitchen to put the prepared food! Using their elbows and facial expressions, the cooks pointed to the dish and then to the name on the menu so we knew which was which because, frankly, it all looked the same.

However, there were only enough menus for one table to order at a time. After about thirty seconds, if they had-n't decided, Marie would come and yank the menus out of their hands.

I somehow ended up in the middle with only one table—a party of two. Which was fine by me.

Since I wasn't that busy, I went into the kitchen to ob-serve the cooks. They were having a great time. I figured they were devouring approximately one meal for every dish they prepared. I wondered what would happen if business picked up. I mean, they might explode.

"You're just standing around," Paolo said. "Why don't you help the girls." I tried to explain that there were three of us servers and only fifteen customers. He still didn't look happy. So I offered to help Sylvie and Anna. "I only have two tables," each said. And they were right. Two tables is not much, even if you are a total zit-brain with no expe-rience. To make Paolo happy I tried to look busy, which can be a challenge for a waiter with only two customers.

The end result of this evening was that the few cus-tomers who accidentally wandered into the establishment reached, I believe, the general conclusion that 100 francs was too much for a small bowl of cold spaghetti covered with tomato paste and lousy service. Also, I was demoted to dishwasher bum. Welcome to France.

Fashion Forward

Fashion Photographer for a Day at the Prêt-à-Porter

PARIS, FRANCE

I NOW KNOW THE DIFFERENCE BETWEEN WIDE-LEGGED hip-huggers and low-waist trapeze skirts. I can tell you which colors any fashion-forward person will be wearing next season and which colors will not be seen until the next retro-look springs forth. I know how to use words like *salon* and *boutique* in their proper contexts. I can pick up any item of woman's clothing and hold it without looking like a total pervert. I am able to ask for directions from a woman wearing nothing but a see-through plastic jacket and some underwear. I can do a pretty good imitation of that bouncy step and spin models do on the catwalk. And I learned that "*haute couture*" is indeed just another pretentious French phrase.

That was just part of my education at the world's largest fashion exposition, Prêt-à-Porter (pronounced "PRET-a por-TAY"), held in a big convention hall on the southern side of Paris. I should note that this is not to be confused with *Prêt-à-Porter*, the movie, or the *haute couture* exposition, which is the supermodel fashion show, also in Paris, depicted in the movie *Prêt-à-Porter.*

I figured that, though it's not as glitzy as the haute couture show, I should attend the Prêt-à-Porter exposition because it has a major impact on the world fashion and, well, I couldn't get into the other one.

I spent my first hour in the Bureau de Presse, which is not a dry-cleaning firm but a little French journalist club at the convention, where, in addition to essential press aids like an open bar, you get a bag filled with heaps of—get ready—fashion literature.

Basically, the way the exhibition works is that designers exhibit their wares (or wears?) in booths like at any other convention. The major difference is that there are jillions of drop-dead gorgeous women walking around in cutting-edge clothing with the surface area of chewing gum wrappers. This makes the convention much more exciting than say, the Book Expo (the only other convention I have ever attended), where overly attractive people are not even allowed in the door.

In my first two hours walking around the convention floor I fell in love at first sight forty times. (Note to wife: Just kidding!) I didn't stare at them openly with my chin dragging on the floor and my tongue leaving a trail of drool or anything, it's just that all the off-duty models seemed to be posing for a photo that no one was taking. Except me. I felt sorry for them. And besides, this was my big chance to be a fashion photographer.

Women were wearing things so revealing, it made them look twice as naked than just being naked. One woman had a top with a low-cut V-neck that went down to her waist and a high-cut skirt that went up to her waist.

Like a stalactite and stalagmite about to join, there were just a few threads around the navel holding the whole out-fit together—a tiny breeze could have blown it off.

I think the trick to wearing and looking good in most of these clothes is to be born a professional model. I don't see how anyone else could possibly fit into them while maintaining normal circulation. The current look is to wear clothing that is about two sizes too small. It's as if all the women confined their shopping to the junior-miss section.

By the way, the big name supermodels wouldn't be caught dead at this show because it is, as the French name implies, ready-to-wear clothing. That means it's the sort of clothing you can just walk into a store and purchase. (I did-n't realize there was any other kind. But apparently there is.) And same-day purchase clothing is, I guess, not serious enough to require big name supermodels.

Big name supermodels are only hired to "catwalk" by big name designers like Coco Chanel. And the big names design *haute couture* clothes, meaning you can't just go into a store and buy them. First you have to take out a mortgage on your house. And even then you can't leave with the clothing. Because it has to be custom made to your size. Now you're thinking, "I can buy an overpriced Chanel bag without having it custom made." And you'd be correct. Big name designers do make ready-to-wear accessories so everyday above-average people like you can barely afford to own some.

I watched two fashion shows on the convention's larger catwalks. The first big show was referred to as "normal" by the people standing behind me, who were wearing trendy lampshades on their heads. Most of the outfits I saw on stage like a bikini made from tiny green mirrors could have been worn by Cher in concert. How practical is that? I mean aside from the fact that it could double as a disco ball when you're not at the beach. And the model wearing it had some green glitter sprayed around her navel. Come to think of it, most of the beachwear models did. Just remember you heard it here first: mirrored swimsuits and navel glitter!

The other fashion show was "alternative," meaning no one, except space aliens and maybe Dennis Rodman, would ever even contemplate wearing this stuff. These models had tattoos, dyed hair, and pierced everything. One female with a shaved head modeled an old t-shirt with a big hole in it that allowed one bare breast to hang out. She also had on a pair of well-used men's briefs with a hole exposing one cheek. (I'm not sure about the copyright laws, but I could swear this innovative design was stolen from a roommate I had in college.) A male modeled a full-body Saran Wrap jumpsuit. Another man wearing a faux-fur dress displayed a large pin that pierced his mouth completely shut. What does all this mean? It means we'll probably see this fashion in a few weeks on Main Street in Boise, Idaho.

As for my personal taste in clothes, I have this to say: Thank God for my press pass, or I'd have been kicked out for a fashion violation. I bought my clothes the usual way: I bought a blue shirt (on sale) at one store and some brown pants (on sale) at a different store. I didn't have any particular fashion statement in mind when I wore these items *ensemble,* beyond covering my chest and *derriere.* Unfortunately, the blue and brown weren't mismatching enough to look like I did it on purpose, so I didn't qualify for "intentional gross mismatching" (another new fashion I witnessed). People with green hair, pierced foreheads, and pantyhose shirts were looking at me same the way I was looking at them.

I asked one woman just to be sure: "My outfit doesn't really match, does it?" "No." "Not at all?" "No." "Thank you for your frank assessment."

The next new style is...beats me. I saw everything on display: from sport coats with vinyl lapels to shirts made out of shag carpet. Pick a fabric and you'd find it here. Sandpaper, origami paper, toilet paper—why not? I saw a few women modeling skimpy dresses with small words written all over them. They looked like giant cheat-sheets for French class.

As far as I can tell, there are only two rules of thumb in the fashion industry. The first is that there is no rule of thumb. The second is that everyone is trying to make a rule of thumb, which is in direct conflict with rule Number One.

According to the fashion literature I picked up at the Prêt-à-Porter press club, here's a hot tip for summer: Keep your eyes out for English Green and Sublime Violet. I'm assuming these are colors.

Having the Last Glass

Working in a Swedish Glass Factory

KOSTA, SWEDEN

FLORIDA HAS THE MAGIC KINGDOM, WILL PERKINS HAS the Wild Kingdom, and Sweden has the Glass Kingdom. There are no overgrown mice walking around on their hind legs or footage of lions munching on zebras, but if your grandmother keeps a bowl of candy in her home, then the Glass Kingdom is probably where it came from. (The jar, not the candy, or your grandmother—unless she's Swedish.)

The Glass Kingdom is an area in southeast Sweden where you can't drive for more than two minutes without running into a glass factory, and breaking it. There are nearly twenty such factories within a twenty-mile range. The undisputed ruler of this kingdom is Orrefors, so naturally I started my job search here.

I thought this might be difficult because my Swedish was not up to scratch, I didn't have a Swedish work visa, and, well, I didn't know the first thing about making glass. But I was eventually passed on to an extremely nice PR

199

person who told me I might be able to try my hand at glass-making for a day, though she suggested it would be more interesting to "work" at Kosta Boda, better known for their avant-garde style. A longtime rival of Orrefors (in fact, Kosta Boda tried to buy Orrefors twenty years ago), Kosta Boda is now owned by the Orrefors Group.

Orrefors is an old Swedish word meaning "Don't forget to bring your wallet"; and *Kosta Boda* means "While you're at it, take out a loan." Some products are affordable for people like you and distant relatives of Bill Gates. But collecting this glassware is normally reserved for the kind of people who let their horses get haircuts from guys named Philippe.

In order to work a full day at Kosta Boda, I was told I would have to wake up at 5:30 A.M. Seeing the stricken look on my face, and since the Glass Kingdom was located several hours from anywhere, they let me spend the night at the Kosta Boda guest house.

I started my brief apprenticeship in the glass-painting department, where they decorate plates, bowls, and glasses with elaborate designs. As you might imagine, this requires considerable skill, and during the first hour I didn't display any. In the second hour, as I gradually woke up, I still didn't display any, but by then I was thoroughly enjoying myself. What I'd do was take, say, a perfectly nice glass bowl, set it next to the predesigned model; let Linda, a professional glass painter, help me mix my paints, and then I'd paint something on the bowl that didn't resemble the predesigned model in the slightest, except for the color scheme, thanks to Linda.

Fortunately, the public relations people, sensing a keen opportunity for publicity, had assigned Karin, a young PR intern, to guide me through the large factory, help with occasional translation, and tell me (with a straight face) that every piece of junk I designed was a masterpiece.

After creatively defacing about $500 worth of fine glass, Karin led me to the engraving department, where I learned how to creatively deface fine glass via the technique of engraving.

There are two general types of engraving. One type can be learned in about a day. The other takes four to five years to master. I nearly got the hang of the first technique, which involves tracing a design on a plate with a dentist's drill. "Incredible," spouted Karin, looking over my shoulder. Naturally, it didn't look like much, but I was really getting into this arts-and-crafts stuff.

Moving on to the second technique, Jan (a master engraver) gave me some valuable pointers. I managed, in just one hour, to engrave a dolphin on a glass vase. If you dimmed the lights and backed up a bit (to, say, Finland), it looked vaguely like a dolphin on a glass vase. If you didn't take these measures, it looked like Charlie the Tuna on a glass vase.

"That's O.K.," mustered Jan.

"It's just beautiful," gushed Karin.

It was time to attend lunch. I mean, a press conference with food. The glass designer, Gunnel Sahlin, was giving a presentation in Swedish for the local press on her recent exhibits in America. In Sweden, a few of these glass designers, Gunnel included, are as known as TV celebrities because, well, people really seem to like glass here. I was introduced to Gunnel but I didn't ask her anything because I hadn't understood much of her hour-long Swedish presentation and I had been nodding my head appreciatively the whole time as if I had.

The next stop, the glass-blowing department, looked like Santa's workshop—if it were moved to a sauna and the elves had taken steroids.

Krister, a master glassblower, tried to show me the ropes. The first step, he said, was to take a long metal blowing rod and get some hot glass on the end of it. I walked over to the large pizza oven and dipped the tip of the rod into a pot of white liquid glass. But I didn't do it quickly enough. At six feet away, the hair on my arms singed from the extreme heat.

I pulled out what looked like a giant glowing (2,000-degree) wad of chewing gum. Then Krister asked me to practice blowing a bubble with it. While spinning the rod quickly to keep the gooey glass from dripping onto the floor, I slowly began to inflate it. With minimal effort, I was able to make a bubble nearly the size of a chair. Before it burst, Krister took the bubble over to a trough of cool water and let it break safely underwater.

"Now," he said, "you will make a bowl." Actually, I made several bowls. But if you saw any of them, I doubt you would say, even if you were trying to be polite, "Hey, nice bowl!" You would probably say, "Hey, nice lopsided ashtray!" or "Hey, nice wad of melted glass!" or simply "Hey!"

Karin loved them all.

We went up to the PR offices to say hello. Karin insisted I show everyone my dolphin vase. "Look, isn't it beautiful!?" They all agreed it was. The head PR person even took a photo of it. My plates and glasses were also passed around. The PR office squealed with each creation: "Beautiful!" "Wonderful!" "Incredible!" Once all my handicraft was spread out, I could see I had ruined an impressive amount of glass.

So what, you may ask, did I take away from this experience besides a hideous set of original tableware? Well, I felt so bad about ruining their glass that I purchased an expensive item for which I have absolutely no use for. But the most amazing thing was that in this same glass shop, which looks like a wedding gift utopia, I found myself picking up large glass objects and examining the painting, engraving, and blowing work for several minutes with the eye of a craftsman. I had acquired expensive taste.

Truffle Hunter

Digging for the Elusive White Fungi in Italy

ALBA, ITALY

LORD BYRON KEPT A TRUFFLE ON HIS DESK FOR inspiration. Kings, princes, and barons have spent their days trying to acquire this delicacy. The famous Italian composer Rossini called it "the Mozart of fungi." The best place to find this precious food flavoring is in the small northwestern Italian town of Alba, the self-proclaimed truffle capital of the world, whose motto is "Where fungi isn't just the white stuff that grows on fraternity carpets over summer vacation!"

Unfortunately, I didn't know the best truffles were found in Alba, which is why I went to France first. My initial plan was to go to the province of Provence and rent a female pig. (Sows are naturally drawn to truffles because they think—and this is true—that truffles smell exactly like sexual hormones excreted by male pigs.)[1]

---

[1] And if that doesn't work up your appetite for truffles, I don't know what will.

However, I heard a few people in Paris say that the best truffles, white truffles, were found in Italy with the help of dogs who have to be specially trained (because they are not normally fond of pig sex-hormone excretions). Naturally, the people who said this were Italian. And dog lovers. But I had the information confirmed by a neutral source—a chef from Switzerland.

In Alba, I learned from locals that there are three basic types of truffles. There's the crude black truffle, which smells approximately like the armpit area of a professional linebacker's t-shirt who may have—at some point in his life—used deodorant. A notch up in quality is the more so-phisticated French Perigord black truffle, which smells like the same shirt after it has been fermenting in an unvented locker for three months. And finally, at the apex of the truf-fle pyramid is the elegant white truffle, which smells like the same shirt two years later, when all that's left is a little scrap of armpit fungus that the cockroaches won't go near.

The friendly ladies at the Alba tourist office managed to link me up with Mr. Teresio, the former president of the Alba Truffle-Hunting Association. They told me that he would take me truffle hunting. However, there must have been a misunderstanding, because he just drove me around his truffle farm (in a car that had a windshield the size of a glove compartment). A kind man in his sixties, Mr. Teresio was growing trees on his land specifically to cultivate truf-fles, which I learned grow underground as parasites on tree roots. I also learned that they range in size from acorn to softball and look just like brain tumors.

Other than that, it wasn't a particularly informative three-hour interview because I couldn't understand a word of his Italian, even though he used hand gestures to help bridge the communication gap. I just nodded and said "*sì*" every time he looked over at me. However, when I tried to say something, usually in a mixture of Spanish and French, he'd interrupt me and say "*Non capisco*" (I don't understand), and start yammering again.

The tour ended at Mr. Teresio's house, where I met his two daughters, both of whom spoke perfect English. I asked one to convey to her father that I would like to actually look for truffles. She translated, and he explained that it was much too early for the white truffle season (although I had heard differently in Alba and had even seen some fresh white truffles for sale). He said that the black truffle area was too far away. But for the purpose of demonstration, he buried a black truffle the size of a tennis ball (that he just happened to have on hand) about two inches under the ground and released his truffle-hunting dogs.

The dogs, who acted as if they had been in captivity since the Renaissance, ran pretty much everywhere, except to where the truffle was. Mr. Teresio tried to help them out by calling them to the spot. One of the dogs just came up and, without realizing it, lay down on the precise spot where the truffle had been buried. (Even I could smell the truffle from that close.) Mr. Teresio called the other dog over to the same spot and pounded the ground. The dog looked quizzically at the ground and then began, in a manner of speaking, to hump the terra firma above the buried truffle. After ten minutes, he told me that these dogs were specially trained to find white truffles, which have a different "perfume."

I returned, disheartened, to the women at the tourist office, who directed me to another tourist office, where I was told that it would be impossible to find someone to take me truffle hunting because it was now too late in the day to locate a truffle hunter.

Just then, a local truffle hunter named Mario Aprile walked in. I asked him (in French, our common language) or, rather, begged him, to take me truffle-hunting. Mario, a junior high school teacher by day, shrugged and brought me back to his house in a nearby village. There I met his wife and son and they gave me—out of the goodness of their hearts—an entire floor of the house to use as my living quarters.

I couldn't help but notice Mario's truffle-hunting trophy collection, which was extremely impressive. I wasn't aware that truffle-hunting was a major sport. In fact, at first glance, I thought maybe I was in the home of a top-seeded professional bowler.

At 11 P.M., it was time to start looking for truffles. Most truffle hunting is done at night because no one likes to give their secret spots away. Selling truffles is handled confidentially as well. This can be observed at the Saturday market in Alba. While I was there, the price for white truffles was around $1,000 per pound, but this price fluctuates weekly because the truffles only stay "fresh" for about ten days. Anyway, the truffle hunters don't want news to spread about big finds in their favorite areas, so they only display a few tiny truffles at the market and keep all the big ones in their pockets. For those who are interested in the better fungi, the transaction is, much like a drug deal, moved to a more private location.

Mario lent me some *stivali* (rubber boots), a *zappetta* (pick), a *lampadina tascabile* (flashlight), and a *bastone* (cane); we put his *cane* (dog) into the back of the *macchina* (car) and drove off to a nearby secret *posto* (spot) to find some *tartufi* (pig sex hormone-flavored fungi). Then we trudged through swampy undergrowth, which was not easy in the dark, until the dog, Biancha, picked up a scent. Biancha was supposed to dig up the truffle, then stop and get a reward from Mario. However, Biancha had a craving for the truffles as well; at least she preferred them to the crackers Mario had brought along as rewards. So as soon as she started pawing at the ground, Mario would rush over to stop her from finding the truffle first.

In two hours, I found—with the help of an award-winning truffle dog and an award-winning truffle hunter—two ping-pong ball-sized truffles worth about $50 each. Mario said this was excellent luck. Sometimes he has looked for days without finding anything.

Truffles may stink, but when thinly—and I'm talking gold-leaf-thin—sliced on pasta in portions the size of parmesan cheese toppings, the sublime flavor makes it well worth the effort. And it didn't hurt that Mario's wife was an amazing cook. She told me the only basic rule of thumb when cooking with truffles was: Don't mix truffles with other strong foods or spices (like garlic) that might mask the flavor. Although I would add the second rule: Make friends with a professional truffle hunter so you can get some for free.

PART SIX

EASY DOES IT

Southfork Fix

Paying to Peek at the Legendary TV Set

DALLAS, TEXAS

I CAN'T REMEMBER WHO SHOT J.R. I FORGET HOW
Bobby managed to come back from the dead and appear in
Pam's shower. And, for the life of me, I have no idea how
Lucy ended up selling Abdominizers on TV infomercials.

But as we drove into Dallas, Signe and I did what just
about everybody does, I presume, when they get to Dallas.
We started humming the theme song to *Dallas,* the TV
show. C'mon, you know the one:

"Da-daa da-daa

Da-daa-da-da-daa-da

Daaa daaa daaa da-da-daaa!"

After "The Star-Spangled Banner" and the Flintstones
theme, it's probably the most unifying song in America—
and the only one that everyone knows the words to.

We looked over at other cars driving down the freeway
and, I swear, entire families were singing it in unison. Or
maybe they were just talking.

After two days in Dallas, the song was so well implanted

in our brains that we had to find some kind of release. We figured there must be a *Dallas* exhibit somewhere in the area. We called information and, sure enough, Southfork, the Ewing clan ranch, was open to visitors.

Southfork, only forty minutes from downtown Dallas, was sold for $12 million in 1984 when the owners became tired of having souvenir-size portions of the ranch removed by aggressive tourists who would later attach the Berlin Wall. The ranch went bankrupt as a tourist attraction, then was picked up for $2.6 million by Rex Maughn, who gave it a $500,000 facelift.

Our singing reached a fever pitch as we approached the Southfork gate but came to an abrupt halt as we caught a glimpse of the famous white ranch house, which was— you'll never guess—much smaller than it looked on TV.

The famous patio swimming pool, for example, was half the size of a boxing ring. How did they film those long swimming scenes? They'd tie an "invisible" plastic cord around the swimmer so, say, Bobby could swim for upwards of a week without ever reaching the other side.

With all the remodeling, the interior looked very nice, but it didn't bear much resemblance to the scenes on TV (most of which were shot in Hollywood on a set three times bigger). It just looked like the expensive house of an alcoholic family, except that there were pictures of Jock, Miss Ellie, J.R., Sue Ellen, Bobby, Pam, and Lucy (doing butt crunches) all over the place.

Most of the rooms were roped off so we couldn't take any ashtrays. We could just peek in from the hallway. Bobby's room looked like you might imagine Bobby's room to look—if he were still in junior high. Same went for Lucy's. But J.R. and Sue Ellen's room was a bit more adult and open to the public. It featured a canopied bed and an adjoining bathroom with very upscale fixtures.

While we were milling around the house, a six-year-old boy on our tour turned to his mother and asked, "Mom, what's a soap opera?" She glanced around at us older people for help and we just gave her that "good luck" look. She finally told him, "It's a TV show where people do stuff to each other." Close enough.

Not far from the house, in one of the larger stables, was a *Dallas* museum, included with the $6.50 tour. The most noteworthy item on display in the almost-barren museum was the prop gun used to pretend to shoot the merciless oil magnate J.R. It was enclosed in the sort of Plexiglas display case normally reserved for rare Egyptian artifacts. This gun, as you may recall, caused the most-discussed cliffhanger episode of the modern era—an event that will stump future anthropologists for millennia to come. Why, they will ask, did the activity in ninety-six countries come to a standstill during the summer of 1980?

My favorite part of the museum, after the video that continued to play the theme music, was the *Dallas* family tree, which looked more complex than the electrical grid of a power plant. All seventy-eight people who ever appeared on the show were listed, including all thirteen of J.R.'s mistresses. Blood connection lines were drawn in red, marriage lines were in blue, flings were in white, and some of the lines came to a dead end with the words: See *Knots Landing*.

The Sound of Muzak

Humming Along with the Famous Austrian Tour

SALZBURG, AUSTRIA

"LET'S GIVE A BIG HAND FOR HINEY THE BUS DRIVER," said Peter the Tour Guide as we—a bus full of Americans, mostly over sixty and toting video cameras—set off on "The Original *Sound of Music* Tour" in our "Comfortable Panorama Bus." We dutifully clapped for Hiney so that he would not do anything rash, like abandon us at the family von Trapp house.

I'm not normally attracted to organized tours and *The Sound of Music* does not rank among my all-time favorite films, but the brochure looked so campy that I thought it could be fun.

Peter, an American himself, stood at the front of the bus and welcomed us over the PA system with the same obnoxiously soothing voice used in airports to page people and explain what the loading and unloading zone is for.

In no time we reached the first stop on the tour, which was not actually a stop. We drove past the "Do Re Mi" Fountain where Maria and the Children danced around and sang.[1] "We could see the 'Do Re Mi' Fountain," Peter explained, "at the end of the tour, on our own."

Peter the Tour Guide then tried a *Sound of Music* quiz of the most esoteric variety. "Who remembers that scene at the abbey where Maria and that other nun were speaking?" Some tourists raised their hands. "And then right after that Maria left the abbey and walked through the woods, remember?" A few raised their hands. "And then she walked over the hillside of that one mountain, right?" One woman raised her hand. "Now here's the question: Does anyone remember the name of that mountain?"

Peter, it seemed, had seen this movie an unhealthy number of times. I had seen it twice, and the last time was about twelve years ago, so there were a lot of fuzzy bits in my memory and I missed most of Peter's references to the film. As did Jeanne, a woman from Chicago who was sitting next to me. But she did know the words to all the songs!

The first actual stop was the house that portrayed the front of the family von Trapp house in the movie. Many of us did not recall this lakeside facade, but Peter assured us that we did. "You remember, the one where the Children were boating on the lake and fell into the water—ha, ha, ha." Then a few kilometers away we saw—but were not able to stop at—the house that was used in the movie as the back of the family von Trapp house. Of course, the interior scenes were all shot in a studio in Hollywood, or maybe London.

We also saw, on the other side of town, the "I Am Sixteen Going on Seventeen" Gazebo that was supposed

---

[1] It was never just "the fountain." Peter always called it the "Do Re Mi Fountain."

to be in the backyard. Two girls on the tour from Minnesota offered to take my picture in front of the gazebo and,
while I was posing with minimal excitement, a retired
American woman on the tour, who was posing for a photo
of her own, decided to serenade me with the "I Am
Sixteen Going on Seventeen" song.

Back on the bus, Peter the Tour Guide[2] told us that
most of the "I Am Sixteen Going on Seventeen" gazebo
scenes were shot in a reconstructed "I Am Sixteen Going
on Seventeen" gazebo in Hollywood, or maybe London,
that was much bigger than this gazebo—which had also
been reconstructed, according to the brochure, "for the
pleasure of those fans still returning after thirty years."

Aside from the fact that most of the movie was shot in
Hollywood or London, not Salzburg, and that people
spoke German in Salzburg, not English, there were several
other noteworthy inconsistencies between the film and the
real-life von Trapp story. For example, the Rolf character
("who fell in love with Liesl, became a Nazi recruit, and
then blew the whistle on the family hiding in the
monastery") was—and this is hard to believe—totally
made up by a Hollywood writer! And the real Maria von
Trapp, according to Peter the Tour Guide, was more like
Roseanne Barr than Julie Andrews; the Children couldn't
stand her. The Baron, who apparently should have been
played by John Goodman, was actually the nice guy.

But perhaps the biggest shocker was that the real von
Trapp family never escaped over the hills to freedom. The
mountain they were escaping over at the end of the movie
was the Vunderberg (for those of you who wanted the an-

---

[2] I decided to call him "Peter the Tour Guide" instead of just "Peter."

swer to Peter's trivia question), which leads into *Germany*. What really happened to the family von Trapp, according to Peter the Tour Guide, was that they escaped on a train to Rome, hopped a ship to America, bought a station wagon, and toured the United States for a year, performing at small concerts, weddings, and bar mitzvahs along the way. That Hollywood took such liberties with the storyline is, also according to Peter the Tour Guide, why no one in Austria wants anything to do with the film.

After these revelations, Hiney the Bus Driver took us about an hour out of Salzburg to Saint Gilgen, a mountain lake resort. On the way, Peter the Tour Guide played the *Sound of Music* soundtrack and invited us to sing along. (Nobody sang along, except Jeanne, a professional singer, and me, not a professional singer, or even a remotely decent singer.) As we disembarked at Saint Gilgen, I asked some of my fellow passengers what this place had to do with the movie or the von Trapp family. No one knew. But several large tourist souvenir shops were set up so that we could buy something to remember we had been there.

I should mention that the older tourists, who made up roughly 90 percent of the group, simply loved Peter the Tour Guide. They thought all his jokes were just a scream. We younger passengers, however, were forced to roll our eyes with each corny line. It got to the point where I worried my eyeballs might become permanently stuck in the looking-at-my-brain position.

We stopped next at Mondsee to see the von Trapp Wedding Church. According to Peter, however, this was not the main attraction in town. The main attraction was Mrs. Braun's apple strudel with hot vanilla sauce, which cost about seven dollars and was conveniently located in a restaurant across the street from the church. Just about everyone took a quick obligatory look at the church, then beelined for Mrs. Braun's as instructed.

You might wonder what Christopher Plummer (the actor who played the baron and has since been knighted Sir Christopher Plummer) and Julie Andrews think of the tour. According to promotional posters pinned up around town, both took the tour themselves. To call their comments vague would be an understatement. Sir Plummer said something like "I took the tour" and Ms. Andrews said, roughly, "Me, too."

The tour was kitschy enough to be entertaining, but just barely. It certainly didn't provide thirty dollars worth of kitsch, which is what I paid. My money would have been better spent on four apple strudels with hot vanilla sauce. Hopefully, though, people will continue to take the tour, because I thought Hiney the Bus Driver was a nice guy and I'd hate to see him lose his job, although considering the nature of the tour, in a few years, he'll probably be driving a reproduction of the original *Sound of Music* tour bus made in Hollywood (or maybe London) and twice as big.

Where the Cows Have No Name

Deciphering a Cattle Auction in Texas

AMARILLO, TEXAS

I COULDN'T TELL YOU THE DIFFERENCE BETWEEN A "cowboy" and a "cowhand," a "steer" and a "steed," or a "hcifer" and a "heifee." I only went to Amarillo's cattle auction hall because I get a kick out of listening to those auctioneers—the only people I've ever heard who can talk more and say less than a room full of presidential candidates.

I entered the parking lot and wedged in my rented Subaru between two dust-covered, shit-kicker Ford pickups. The Amarillo auction hall was, at one time, the biggest in the world. Now that title is held by an auction hall in Oklahoma, and thanks to the TV Cattle Auction Channel (aka Pay-Per-Cow), live cattle bidding here is not quite what it used to be.

The 300-seat auction hall was about a third full when I arrived. There was a curved "catwalk" for the animals to show off their loins with an entry gate on the left, an exit gate on the right, and several cowboys (or cowhands) to help usher them in the right direction.

I was the only person in the auction hall who was wearing sandals and not wearing jeans. My belt buckle was so wimpy, it could have been beaten up by a Texan cuff link. Any one of these dress code violations would probably have been enough to get me arrested as a whale-hugging communist. But, to top it off, I didn't even have a goddamn, born-in-the-USA, step-aside-son-I-gotta-spit STETSON!

A Stetson is the Coca-Cola of cowboy hats, the lederhosen of the wild west. Madeleine Albright wears one. The Marlboro Man wears one. And nearly every man in the auditorium sat in the shade of one.

I spent the first hour trying to figure out the bidding signs, many of which are so subtle you could miss them even if you were looking right at the person making the bid. I was afraid to scratch my nose, sneeze, or blink for fear I'd end up the owner of an expensive steer, or perhaps even a steed.

Some bidders had complicated hand and arm gestures that looked like...well, I'm a little rusty with my baseball signals, but I'm pretty sure one guy was trying to get a cow to steal third.

The cow herself, obviously not a baseball fan, was equally confused. She just ran back and forth between the gates as if the two cowhands had her trapped in a pickoff between bases. In desperation, she stopped in the center and relieved herself. The auctioneer hammer came down with a bang. She was out!

At one point, four female tourists who looked like recent graduates of the Holy Princess Junior League College for Texas Debutantes entered the auction hall and proceeded down to the front row. Every Stetson turned. The auctioneer briefly stopped talking. Even the cattle stopped to watch them, though they were probably just blinded by the jewelry. The ladies' four pairs of cowboy boots were worth, cumulatively, more than my rental car. I gathered this was how auction-hall tourists were supposed to look.

Trying to learn more about the auction, I turned to Bo, a serious-looking cowboy sitting next to me. Some of the bidders, he explained, were "traders," who might buy cattle, rent space for them right at the auction house, then sell them the next week and stick around to help bid up the price. Others were "feeders." They typically buy steers when they're small, feed them for about 160 days, then sell them when they've put on some weight, hopefully for a profit. Bo was just looking to pick up a few "head."

The animals were either sold by the "head," by the "pound," or by the "quarter-pound with cheese."

During intermission, I got a chance to speak with Dale Cooper, one of the auctioneers with turbo-charged vocal chords. I expressed interested in his locution skills and he offered to give me a lesson in "calling." Well, to say it was a lesson would be stretching things a bit. He just wanted me to practice saying: "Give-me-twenty-give-me-thirty-twenty-thirty-O.K.-thirty-give-me-forty-thirty-give-me-forty."

I would say: "Give me twenty. Give me thirty. Twenty. Thirty. Forty, give me thirty. I mean, forty give me sixty. No, wait. Sixty, give me forty."

"No," Dale would say. "More like this." Then he'd say it again. And I'd watch very closely to see if he was taking air in through his ears.

"What's the trick?" I asked him.

"Practice." Then, as an afterthought—perhaps as a rebuke for not wearing a Stetson—he said, "And learn your numbers."

According to Dale, "A caller is like a pitcher. The auction owner might walk out and pull you if you're not getting the big bids in." Madison Michener, the owner of the Amarillo auction, agreed that this happens, but said he doesn't do it. He noted that a strong caller (or a caller on a roll) can average about 20 percent higher prices.

"A caller is really just a fast-talking salesman," explained Dale.

I didn't make much progress towards an auctioneering career, but I was content to sit back and watch this entertaining American institution. Although three hours without scratching my nose, sneezing, or blinking was about as much as I could handle.

Leading a Puppet to Water

Catching a Vietnamese Water Puppet Show

HANOI, VIETNAM

WATER PUPPETS. SOUNDS LIKE SOME KIND OF FAILED Christmas toy. Or an ornate set of fishing lures available exclusively on the Home Shopping Network. Or maybe a made-for-TV movie in which a U.S. Navy-trained team of Muppets guest star on *Sea Quest*.

Think again. In Vietnam, water puppets are part of a very serious and ancient performing art that is still widely practiced today. Although some claim that this offers at least partial explanation for why U.S. action movies are now extremely popular in Vietnam.

Originating in the Nam Ha province in northern Vietnam, this special brand of puppeteering has spread throughout the country over the years, reaching its commercial zenith in Hanoi, where the three-story Municipal Water Puppet Theater out-neons every other architectural eyesore in town.

I had no idea what to expect as I made my way to the theater, but several questions came to mind: Should I bring a swimsuit? Would the audience need to tread water? And what sort of credentials are required in this line of work? PADI certification? Synchronized swimming?

When I arrived at the ticket window, I decided I'd spoil myself a little. Jump up a social class or two. Join the elite of Hanoi. I opted for the premium-class tickets...for $3.

The 300-seat theater looked completely sold out for this performance. I grabbed a chair in the second row next to an Austrian journalist named Gerhardt. On the other side of me was an XXL French woman traveling with a French tour group that took up the rest of the row and the two rows behind it (they all had matching yellow handbags and hats with the name of the tour company). Just as the performance started, a massive German tour group (who somehow managed to out-underdress the French) passed in front of the stage, obstructing our view for the first five minutes, so I'm afraid I'm unable to tell you how the show began.

After the German migration ended, I could see the illuminated stage, a two-story pagoda with a rectangular kiddy pool in front of it. A three-foot-tall puppet was standing in the center of the pool, shin deep in water. He appeared to be controlled by a metal pole attached to his feet just under the water's surface and operated from behind the pagoda. The puppet was ivory white, fitted with two black pigtails jutting out at valley-girl angles, and wearing a gold loincloth—presumably cutting-edge water puppet fashion.

Then a water buffalo puppet wandered out and the puppet man seemed to either use it to plow an imaginary field or dance around with it. I couldn't quite tell. They were soon replaced by other puppet men who fished for puppet fish that were replaced by puppet serpents that swam around and spat water. I was having a rather difficult time following the story line. If I'd been able to understand the traditional Vietnamese singing that accompanied the show, I'm sure it all would have made perfect sense. But without translation, I was as confused as Jean-Claude Van Damme in an acting class.

Gerhardt suggested that the short sketches were meant to depict normal scenes from everyday Vietnamese life. However, since most of the characters were up to their knees in water, it looked like they were depicting everyday life during a monsoon.

We probably weren't the only ones missing the finer points of the performance. Out of the 300 people in the audience, roughly 300 of them were tourists. (Perhaps the Vietnamese were home watching *Rambo*.) Without a single water puppet afficionado among us, we were faced with the immediate and awkward dilemma of not knowing when we were supposed to clap. Just to be safe, we clapped after every act, and sometimes at specific extraordinary displays in between (such as when the serpent puppets spit up water).

As you are probably beginning to gather, this was a *tremendously* exciting performance that kept most of us on the edge of our seats. Unfortunately, in my case, I was on the wrong edge. Having just arrived in Vietnam the same morning, I was recovering from jet lag. About fifty minutes into the performance, lulled by the lovely Vietnamese music, I fell asleep with my head in my right hand, braced on the armrest.

I'm not entirely clear about what happened next, but it seems my head slipped out of my hand and I tumbled over, my face plummeting straight into the lap of Mrs. XXL, who let out a shriek that woke me and startled the surrounding audience members—much to the amusement of

Gerhardt, who couldn't stop laughing for the remaining ten minutes of the show. Between Gerhardt's laughing and my profuse apologies to the woman, I didn't catch the ending of the show, so I can't tell you about that part either.

To get a little more insight into this ancient craft, I thought I'd try my hand at water puppeteering. So I made an appointment to meet with the theater's director, Mr. Le Van Ngo, the following morning.

Mr. Le Van Ngo arrived for our meeting at 9 A.M. with a translator, a nice young woman who seemed like a capable translator, except when it came to translating. In response to my first question about the early water puppeteering being performed on river banks in the eleventh century, she had a short discussion with Mr. Le Van Ngo and came back with this response: "Already name has water puppet." Nearly every word I uttered produced a look of profound confusion on her face. Thanks to her, Mr. Le Van Ngo believes to this day that I'm a total moron.

When I asked if I could have a go with the puppets, Mr. Le Van Ngo shook his head. "Not qualified," he said. I produced my scuba diving certification card. He studied it for several minutes together with the translator, then shook his head a second time. Via the translator, he informed me that water puppeteering requires three years of university education plus two years of apprenticeship before you get to work the puppets during the show. I spent another fifteen minutes trying to explain that I didn't want to work the puppets during the show; I just wanted a better understanding of the technique.

"No," he kept telling me.

"Why not?" I finally asked.

"Secret."

"What secret?"

"Puppet secret."

The translator confirmed that the technical handling of the water puppets is a trade secret.

I promised I wouldn't run off and start my own water puppet show or sell the secret on the *Sesame Street* black market. But I don't believe this got translated as I had hoped, because Mr. Le Van Ngo got up and left me sitting there with the translator, who didn't seem to find this development the slightest bit odd. We sat there in awkward silence for a while, then I asked if Mr. Le Van Ngo was coming back.

"Not today," she said.

Splash Down

Transit Passengers Hit Iceland's Thermal Springs

REYKJAVIK,  ICELAND

THE FIRST TIME I WENT TO ICELAND I NEVER LEFT THE airport. Looking out the window, I could see that there was, in fact, nothing to see. The visibility at the airport was three feet.

Icelandic Air has long offered some of the best rates to Europe. The $50 or so in savings, I now realize, they hope to make up in the airport during the mandatory layover. As I waited for my connecting flight, bought a $3 cup of hot chocolate, and gawked at the ridiculous prices of the duty free shop where, I should point out, you can buy—in addition to the usual duty-free chocolates and liquors and cigarettes—the local specialty: meat. Icelandic cow is available in chunks the size of tree stumps. Just the sort of thing you want to toss into your carry-on luggage.

My second trip to Iceland lasted slightly longer—four hours. Apparently the Iceland Bureau of Tourism was worried that transit passengers (who, I think, make up the majority of Iceland's tourists) weren't getting a comprehensive view of Iceland because we weren't leaving the airport. So they decided to arrange a complimentary tour for us.

This particular day it was snowing very hard and Iceland looked just like most people imagine—a giant unflavored snowcone. They loaded forty of us onto a bus and we followed a snowplow for twenty minutes to the Blue Lagoon, which is one of Iceland's most famous tourist attractions. I believe this is largely due to the fact that it's only twenty minutes from the airport.

If Blue Lagoon conjures up an image of Brooke Shields parading around a tropical island wearing little more than her eyebrows, you'll be a little disappointed by this place. The Icelandic Blue Lagoon is a Wimbledon centre-court-sized rocky pool that was formed during the construction of a thermal energy plant. While drilling into the earth's core, someone accidentally uncorked an aquifer of unnaturally blue water, which spilled over and made a rather toxic-looking pond.

So Icelanders made this lemon into lemonade. Or, to be more accurate, they made this radioactive-looking pool into a swimming pool. They built a fence around the accessible part (the part not obstructed by the energy plant), printed up some color brochures about its health benefits, and charged admission to swim there.

Icelandic Air picked up the admission fee, but most of us forgot to pack a swimsuit and towel in our carry-on bags. We had to fork over $4 to rent them—conveniently payable in any currency.

Surprisingly, just about everyone decided to suit up. But instead of Brooke Shields, I got to see transit passengers wearing rented swimsuits—a sight almost as unnatural as the color of the water. The staff had carefully distributed the swimsuits so that no one received one that actually fit. I was wearing a turquoise Speedo I had not seen the likes of since junior high, and hope I don't see again for at least as long.

The air temperature was 10 degrees below zero, it was snowing like mad, and we were all shivering. So naturally we jumped into the thermal water. "I think someone forgot to turn on the thermal part," one of my fellow passengers said. It was indeed about as warm as the rest of Iceland.

I tried to swim around to stay warm, but I kept thinking that if I swam out too far, I might just get sucked into one of the energy plant's turbines. Everyone else, I noticed, was keeping a safe distance as well.

Except for one Danish man with abundant natural body insulation, no one stayed in the water for more than five minutes before fleeing to the hot showers and souvenir lounge, where we found, in round numbers, six billion postcards of the Blue Lagoon shot from the one obscure angle that shows neither the energy plant, the gift shop, nor the locker rooms.

As soon as we boarded our plane for New York, I had a different relationship with my fellow passengers. We had overcome Passengers-Anonymous Syndrome, that code of the elevator, subway, bus, and commuter train—no matter how close you stand, no matter how amicable someone may seem, never make eye contact and never ever initiate a friendly conversation.

As I walked down the aisle to my seat, every face looked familiar. I had seen them all in swimsuits—or less. It was a little unnerving. We bonded in a way I only thought possible between hijack victims. Come to think of it, in a way we had been hijacked. We were taken to the Blue Lagoon, we were pressured into donning rented swimsuits, and we were led into a pool of cold water during a blizzard. Regular hijackers just shoot you and get it over with.

Bear Check

Truck Talking across America

MINNEAPOLIS, MINNESOTA

I'D LIKE TO TELL YOU ABOUT A RADIO SHOW CALLED *Truck Talk,* which is nothing like *Car Talk,* the popular and funny NPR program in which two brothers from "Bahwsten" spend 70 percent of their airtime laughing hysterically at their own jokes.

Truck Talk features real truckers discussing real trucking issues that go to the very core of contemporary trucking, such as whether the female driver approaching in the left lane has nice legs.

You probably haven't heard this radio show because you need a special radio to listen to it. The only reason I know this is because I recently spent three months driving around America with Signe. Before we set off, we went to a Radio Shack in Minnesota and purchased—for only $60—a totally worthless CB radio. Of course, we didn't know it was totally worthless until we tested it on the open road. We soon discovered that this radio—which looked like a walkie-talkie—had a range (measured in yards) of about ten (coincidentally, the exact I.Q. of the salesperson who sold it to us).

To make contact with a trucker, we had to pull right up alongside the truck. At that point we might as well have rolled down our window and yelled. In fact, it would have been much easier, because to get within range, we had to fully extend the antenna three yards. And to do that, we had to stick it out the window. When you're going 70 miles per hour, a three-yard antenna bends like a Kmart fishing rod pulling in a forty-pound salmon, which makes it difficult to hold onto the radio and even harder to hear over the truck engine and the antenna whistling in the wind.

So we went to a CB specialty store located in a truck stop just outside of Denver. Here we met Bill, who actually knew something about CBs. Rather a lot. One look at all the electronic gizmos in his office told you he was the sort of person who could take a blender apart, put the pieces back together, and have a piece of equipment that would be a valued addition to a military communications satellite. And still be able to process food.

Bill told us that what we needed was a roof-mounted magnetic antenna and a CB with more power. That's precisely what we got. So we traded in our new yet totally worthless Radio Shack model plus $40 for a used but "tweaked and tuned," very cool-looking Cobra CB and a magnetic roof-mounted antenna called L'il Wil.

We turned on our Cobra, which we had connected to L'il Wil, and when it came to life we heard...static. Really loud static. Then we adjusted the "Squelch" dial and the static was replaced by people speaking, sometimes in complete sentences with correctly conjugated verbs. I can only describe the experience like swimming around in a pool for years and then finally putting on some goggles and having a whole new underwater world open up. Of course, the last time I used goggles in a swimming pool all I saw was floating chunks of armpit deodorant, but that's beside the point.

There was a lot of random chatter—something like a radio version of an Internet chat room, but less focused. Some truck drivers' CBs had longer ranges than small radio stations and others had installed a dramatic echo effect that made them sound like the voice of God, assuming, of course that God has a very pronounced Southern accent.

Usually the chatter was in some kind of code that I was not able to decipher even though I saw *Smokey and the Bandit* twice. So we pulled off at a truck stop outside Saint Louis in the hope of finding a friendly, lingo-savvy trucker. First we met Jeff from Cleveland, but he wasn't much help. He was too intellectual. He had a CB, but he never turned it on because he only listened to educational cassettes. "You can get the wrong impression of truckers from listening to that thing. There's some interesting people on the road, but you're not likely to meet them with a CB."

Then we met a bearded and well-tattooed man in a stained tank top who introduced himself as Five-Timer (five ex-wives). He invited us to follow him on the road so we could practice using the CB while we drove. An "alligator," he explained, is a blown-out tire sitting on the side of the road. A "chicken coup" is a truck-weighing station. A "four wheeler" is a car. A "condo" is a truck with a large living cabin. A "lot lizard" is a prostitute who frequents truck stops. And I'm glad he told us that "good buddy" is now a derogatory term for a homosexual, because I had been saying it all across Nebraska.

Perhaps the most useful aspect of the CB lexicon is the word *bear*, which comes in several breeds: "smokey" (state trooper), "county mountie" (county sheriff) and "local yokel" (guy from Village People who dresses like a police officer). When used properly, a CB can be more accurate than a fuzz buster. The way it works is that you ask people coming from the other direction for a "bear check." Then they'll tell you at which mile marker the police are waiting.

While Five-Timer was teaching us CB lingo, he should have been filling his tank. He ran out of gas. So we picked him up and drove him to the nearest gas station—our first radio-aided emergency service. It must have been pretty humiliating for a professional trucker to have to squat in the back of a rented Subaru with several days' worth of fast-food wrappers, but he was a good sport about it. Especially after we promised not to tell anyone.

I mostly used the CB for asking slow truckers to get out of the left lane so I could pass. This was a bit tricky because any eighteen-wheeler could run my four-wheeler into a chicken coup and I'd need a 10-38 and a 10-37 to get my head out of my 10-65.

In Florida, our Cobra shorted out. We had to pay $20 to have another CB specialist named CW (real name: CW) do something to it with a soldering iron. He recommended we also replace the cable so that it wouldn't happen again. We did, for only $10. That brought my running CB tab to $130.

Even with our fully functioning Cobra, it was still hard to get any real conversation going. I tried to start a dialogue on the Middle East peace process. I solicited opinions on welfare. I even asserted various political slogans. Nothing. After 6,000 miles and fourteen states, Signe came up with an enlightened idea: We'd have a discussion with each other and see who would chime in.

Me: Lady, what you wearin'? [Hand receiver to Signe.]

Signe: Nothing. [Hand receiver back to me.]

Me: Can I have your phone number, you sexy little thing? [Hand receiver to Signe.]

Signe: Sure.

Trucker Number One: Don't give your phone number to that jerk, give it to me.

Trucker Number Two: No, give it to me.

Using this technique, we engaged a number of truckers around the country in deep conversation. Well, O.K. not that deep. But it was still more entertaining than listening to most small-town DJs.

Waiting for the Adipose Lady to Sing

A Night at the Opera in Vienna

VIENNSTRIA

NORMALLY I WON'T GO NEAR AN OPERA. IT'S NOT THAT I hate the music. I don't. In fact, I find it relaxing. The problem is I have a hard time relaxing knowing I had to cough up $60 for my ticket. For that price, if relaxation is the aim, I could get a professional massage.

Only once did I find an opera ticket price I could relate to, and, surprisingly, it was in Vienna, Austria, at the State Opera House (Staatsoper). It sounded too good to be true; I thought I had miscalculated the exchange rate. I checked again, then bought a ticket to see an opera in the world's most famous opera house for a little over four dollars. Entrance into Mozart's stomping ground for the price of a chicken chimichanga and medium Slurpee.

There was one minor drawback: My ticket was standing-room only…for four hours. At least I wouldn't nod off in the middle of the performance.

I went back to my youth hostel to dig some clean clothes out of my backpack. There weren't any. So I took off my jeans, shook them vigorously, and put them back on. I didn't have time to shower; I just applied deodorant—generously. Then I grabbed my wrinkled oxford and tried to "iron" it with the time-honored technique of tucking the shirttails deep into my pants until the fabric was pulled taut, then cinching my belt to secure them. I ran out the door.

When I arrived at the opera house's cheap section, I realized I wasn't the only opera-goer living out of a backpack. There were about five of us representing the Great Unwashed. We shifted our weight from one worn sandal to the other, waiting for the show to get started.

To take the weight off my legs, I occasionally rested my head and arms on the guardrail. To the untrained observer, it might have appeared as if I was napping. I wasn't. At least, I don't think so. Otherwise I wouldn't have caught the following snippets of the program.

This opera began with a man wearing tights pretending to chop an imaginary tree with an imaginary ax. He was joined by a male friend, also wearing tights, who burst onto the stage with something very important to say but stopped himself and sang, I think, a *forte-libress al fresco*.[1]

Then some women walked onstage and pretended not to see the men squatting behind the imaginary tree. They sang a scandalous *radicchio al dente* that the men were not

[1] The biggest problem with opera is following the story line. Since they're not singing in English, you have to rely on the acting to figure out what's going on. And as it turns out, these are singers, not actors, so you have to be really patient with them.

supposed to overhear, judging from their overacted expressions, which we could see even though our view was blocked by the imaginary tree.

After two intermissions plagued by expensive drinks and long lines for the toilet, the main guy wearing tights put on a hat with horns sticking out the sides, only to find out that the women had countered this threat by donning a metal breast-plate. So, naturally, he decided to kill himself (the climax). Fortunately, he sang a *mezzanine-soprano al pacino* just before he took the poison, which provided just enough time for one of the women to return all the way from, I believe, backstage to stop him.

They fell in love instantly, decided to get married, and celebrated by—brace yourself—singing.

This was when the clap marathon began. First, the extra opera stars bowed, then the supporting opera stars, then the two main stars, then the female star and the conductor. Then they motioned for the first violinist to bow, but he was too modest and motioned for the opera stars and the conductor to bow again, which they did.

Then the conductor motioned for some musicians in the back to stand up so people could see them for the first time and this caused everyone to clap even more.

The violinists clapped for each other by waving their bows around.

The conductor and the opera stars left and we all had to clap real hard so that they would come right back and we could clap for them some more.

Without missing a beat, they came back. The conductor made all the musicians and opera people bow again. They were all clapping for each other or symbolically waving their instruments around.

Then the opera stars blew some kisses to the crowd, held hands with the conductor, and bowed at the same time. This sent everyone into an absolute unrestrained frenzy of clapping.

Finally, my prayers were answered and the house lights came on. This herd of aristocrats started filing out through the lobby, their hands bright red. Some of the older patrons who descended from the box seats had even broken a sweat. Now, I can understand fifteen minutes of clapping if you paid four dollars for admission. But for the patrons who shelled out sixty bucks, that's a lot of work.

The Connoisseurs

Tagging Along on a Wine-Tasting Tour in South Africa

CAPE TOWN, SOUTH AFRICA

I USED TO ASSOCIATE WINE TASTING WITH THE SORT OF people who have tea sets worth as much as their cars and live in up-market homes like Buckingham Palace. But vineyards in South Africa are helping to change this, and many of today's tasters would not think it strange to go sample wines, then catch a professional wrestling match and a few garage sales on the way home.

Even if I couldn't tell a *cabernet sauvignon* from a *pinot noir* from a *Château Miller Lite*, I thought it would be fun to visit some of the world-class vineyards only thirty minutes outside Cape Town. I wasn't anxious to join a tour group, but the idea of drunk driving seemed even less appealing.

My tour group was under the care of Susha, a twenty-three year old who was oozing attitude from his Ray-Bans, pressed khakis, and tennis shirt, which bore a professional tour company emblem that matched the emblem on our twenty-four-passenger bus.

We had a new breed of wine tasters on board. There was Barney, a sixty-five-year-old Israeli with a Hawaiian shirt, and his traveling companion Eileen, a sixty-year-old South African woman who explained to anyone who would listen that she was not a tourist. As soon as they boarded, they went straight to the back of the bus and started making out.

I sat between Chow, a Taiwanese businessman with a death grip on his camera; Phil, a semiretired British Telecom techie who could, with a single look, bore forty people to death; and Leo, a rotund, geeky, but extremely amicable American mechanical engineer. Behind me was a cute seventy-year-old Scottish couple who introduced themselves to everyone as Mrs. Johnson and Mr. Bone. The other sixteen seats were empty.

Like most bus tour guides, Susha had been trained to drive while spewing mindless trivia into his clip-on microphone. On those few occasions when he didn't have a historical, meteorological, or purely numerical fact on hand, he'd say things like "Up ahead is the Berg River Valley, which gets its name from the Berg River, which runs through it."

Our first stop was Paarl, "one of the wine growing regions and home of the stinkwood tree." We stopped at a monument dedicated to the Afrikaans language—giant, Mapplethorpe-inspired concrete erections. They couldn't have been anything else. It was hard to keep a straight face as I posed for a photo in from of them with Chow.

Then we were off to the world's largest winemaker and distributor Kooperatiewe Wynbouersvereninging van Suid-Afrika Beperk. It's so big (both the name and the company) that the government has forbidden KWV (as they affectionately call it) to sell wine within South Africa because it would so easily dominate the market. Instead, all the KWV's products are for export only, except for a few items conveniently available for sale to tourists. Imagine that!

Our KWV guide introduced herself as Maya-Friedrich and escorted us to a small theater to watch a twenty-minute movie on wine making. Not surprisingly, the entire thing was a commercial for KWV. I learned, for example, that "KWV is a dynamic business organization which, through its marketing company, KWV International, markets internationally." The film showed lots of guys in white coats looking tenderly at grapes as if to say, "We're trained scientists and everything, but we just love the grapes at KWV."

On our walking tour, we could get a scope of KWV's size. It looked like a storage facility for Shell Oil. There were giant tanks everywhere and about 16 jillion oak wine barrels. Most had a normal barrel shape, but some looked like Jacuzzis. The biggest one weighed, when full, "as much as a Boeing 747." We were allowed to look inside one of the smaller barrels. I was the first in line. I took a quick peek and started to wander off.

"What's it like?" asked Mrs. Johnson eagerly.

I could only find the words, "Well, like a barrel."

When it occurred to me that I had paid $50 for a wine-tasting tour that, after three hours, had not yet provided me with so much as an eyedropper of liquid, I politely indicated my thirst to Mrs. Maya-Friedrich. I noticed she was not so fond of my question. Well, maybe not the question. Apparently we should not have been calling her Mrs. Maya-Friedrich, which I had thought was just one of those hyphenated contemporary-marriage names. She explained in exasperation that her first name was Maya and her surname was Friedrich.

I was the only one who thought our gaffe was funny. Chow, however, saw me laugh; thinking he had missed a joke and trying to be polite, laughed as well. Then, because Chow has one of those hysterical wheezing laughs, everyone started laughing. Except Maya Friedrich.

Then (finally!) came the wine tasting. Chow tried just one wine. Mrs. Johnson and Mr. Bone didn't have any. Barney and I were the only ones who tasted all nine varieties. Another tour group with several enthused drinkers was crowding the bar, so I wasn't able to get a good look at which wine was being poured into my glass. As a result, the only thing I can tell you about the nine bottles of wine was that they were all pretty good, except the red wine that came from the second bottle from the left.

After the KWV tour, Susha tried to take us to lunch, but we protested that we wanted to hit another vineyard first. Actually, I was the only one who protested. The others didn't seem that interested in wine. Barney and Eileen were busy in the back seat, Mr. Bone and Mrs. Johnson were sitting quietly, and Chow was taking pictures through the window.

Phil and Leo nodded their consent at my suggestion and that was enough for Susha. We stopped at a smallish château, but Susha said we had to hurry because we were behind schedule. Leo, Phil, Barney, and I went straight for the wine tasting, chugged the five small samples they gave us, jumped back on the bus, and discussed the wines there. ("Did you like the merlot?" "Which one was that?")

After a pricey tourist lunch, we stopped at a vineyard in the Franschoek region, downed some more wine on the palm tree-lined front lawn, and tried to fall asleep on the bus, which was only made difficult by the fact that Susha was still talking into the microphone.

Roughly twenty minutes later, we were woken up and urged to catch the last attraction of the tour—a museum about the Huguenots, who were not French space pioneers who landed in Africa when their spaceship, *The Baguette*, veered off course during a mission, as I had explained to Chow. They were religious refugees from France who knew how to make much better wine than the Dutch. After a few minutes in the museum, we started getting drowsy and convinced Susha to take us back to Cape Town.

Never-Never Land

Kicking Back on the Sinai Peninsula

DAHAB, SINAI PENINSULA, EGYPT

IF THE SOMNOLENT RED SEA COASTAL TOWN OF DAHAB ever worked up enough energy to produce a travel brochure, it would read something like this: "Come to Dahab and do absolutely nothing for a very affordable price! Applying sunscreen is considered an aerobic activity here and loitering is our national sport. No reservations necessary, and don't bother booking a return flight!"

Dahab is *the* traveler's hangout in the Middle East—something like an Arab Never-Never Land. Hundreds of backpackers, Israeli soldiers on holiday, and young Egyptian men trying to score with Western women arrive and depart every day. It takes a while to get the hang of moving that slowly. (Peter Pan and Tinkerbell would definitely require Valium.) The quickest way to fit in would be to die and get reincarnated as a sloth.

I arrived thinking, like many budget backpackers, that I would spend a day in Dahab. And, like most of these visitors, I ended up staying nearly a week. Which is better than the people who came for a week and stayed for a month. Or the ones who came for two weeks in 1982 and are still here. I call this the Dahab Effect. It's actually a mathematical formula. You simply multiply the time you plan to stay by the length of your hair in centimeters and that should give you the approximate amount of time it will take your parents to contact the American Embassy to report you missing.

So what is there to do in Dahab that lures and entraps travelers like the singing sirens of Greek mythology? Nothing! And that's the attraction. Of course, the problem with doing nothing at all is that it's hard to know when you're finished. ("Are you done yet?" "I'm not sure.") That's why people stay so long. When there's a museum to see or a mountain to climb, you know when you're through. When there's nothing to start, there's nothing to finish: to "do" Dahab right, you have to "veg out" until you're sprouting broccoli from your armpits.

It would be an injustice to describe the activities in Dahab using anything but the passive voice.

The entire beach was covered by Bedouin tent cafes, which were sat in by budget travelers for whom noses were pierced. Food was consumed, mango-flavored slush drinks were drunk, backgammon was played, hash was smoked, sex was had, and occasional words were exchanged while harassment was inflicted by eight-year-old Bedouin girls in the form of bracelet selling, which was relentless. Every now and then, souvenirs were purchased and short camel tours were given. More frequently, though, snorkeling gear was rented and fish were looked at while hallucinations occurred in the minds of the people by whom the snorkeling gear was rented. Time was perceived to have stood still, days were thought to have slipped by unnoticed, and concern for this was not felt by anyone.

What the lodgings lacked in quality, they made up for in creative names. Most were honest enough to abandon the traditional rating system. They simply called themselves camps. There was Camp Mohammed Ali, Kangaroo Camp, and Camp I Can't Believe I'm Still Fucking Here. I stayed in a place called, comically, the Hilton Hotel. It was the inverse reciprocal of a five-star hotel. The rooms were essentially tool sheds, complete with padlocks for the door but strictly BYOL.[1] The furniture consisted of a mattress about as thick as my passport, and there were at least three extended families of cockroaches sharing my bed. The joke is that I stayed there for six days—I was too relaxed to seek out more pleasant digs.

For people who manage to snap out of their daytime trance, the evening offers the excitement of the Black Prince disco. Drivers of pickup trucks offer free rides to the Disco, a kilometer and a half away, knowing they'll make their money on the return fare. It's a brilliant marketing concept and I can't figure out why airlines haven't adopted it yet.[2]

One of the most bizarre aspects of Dahab was the fish aspect. Or lack thereof. Unfortunately for the fish and the people who'd like to see them, locals and tourists had covered most of the reef with plastic bags, bottles, and old tires. Rather unsurprisingly, most of the fish had left. I only managed to find one colorful specimen (a parrot fish) when I

---

[1] Bring your own lighting.

[2] Here's how it works: Announce free trips to, say, Australia.
Everyone goes. Then charge triple standard fare for the return trip.

was snorkeling the reef. I swam up close to admire its rose, indigo, and emerald scales. Suddenly, a barbed metal spear shot right through the parrot fish. It keeled over and sank to the bottom of the reef like a speared parrot fish sinking to the bottom of a reef. A skin diver dove down, collected the fish in his bag, and swam off like a skin diver diving down, collecting a fish in his bag, and swimming off. There was nothing left to see.

I spotted the parrot fish that night, along with five others, on a bed of ice in front of a restaurant. There's really no point in trying to see the fish in the ocean. All the best ones are on display each evening—and they're ready to eat! I tried to discuss the fragile ecosystem of the reef with a restaurant owner, using such persuasive arguments such as, "Killing all the fish may affect your snorkeling business."[3] But I may as well have been speaking English to a Bedouin. Well, maybe that was the problem.

I left after six days with a resting heart rate of six beats per minute. My only accomplishment in that time, aside from getting out of bed once a day, was working up a new tourism slogan for Dahab: "The next time you want to do nothing special, make a special trip to do nothing—in Dahab!"

---

[3] He was renting snorkeling equipment right next to the dead fish and saw no irony in this.

Epilogue

DOING WHAT NEEDS TO BE DONE

Learning to Face the Inevitable

SOME TRAVELERS CAN GET GASTROINTESTINALLY traumatized by just thinking about the street food in under-developed countries. Others have to actually go there and eat it themselves. But the real fear that grips travelers venturing into far-flung lands is not necessarily an unsettled stomach or the potentially shoddy medical care that may accompany it, but bathrooms that do not share Martha Stewart's criteria for proper sanitation—or even Attila the Hun's. And by no accident, these countries have restrooms that make our plastic Porta-Potties look like luxury spa resorts.

I've discovered two standard kinds of Third World thrones and, believe me, you wouldn't want to use either of them. So when you have to spend more time doing something in a place where you don't want to do it at all, what do you do? What don't you do? Or, should I say, how do you doo?

The first kind, the squatter, looks like Chief from *One Flew over the Cuckoo's Nest* just picked up the toilet, threw it out the window, and ran from the scene, leaving a six-inch-diameter hole in the floor right where the commode is supposed to be. The idea is that you are supposed to squat over the hole and, like a B-2 bomber, hit the target.

249

The obvious danger is losing your balance and falling backward into an area that I'd just as soon not describe since you may have just eaten sausages with your breakfast. This does happen occasionally because there is nothing to hold on to. The less apparent danger is that squatting causes your pants pockets to become somewhat inverted, so your valuables go sliding irretrievably down the hole. And if this doesn't sound challenging enough, just try reading a newspaper at the same time. Remember, you'll also have to hold a flashlight in your mouth since these lavatories don't have decent lighting or, sometimes, any lighting at all.

Managing all this requires a number of skills, none of which fell within the scope of my liberal arts degree— which, for lack of toilet paper, would have really come in handy.

Lack of toilet paper?! Yes, that's correct. A very large portion of the world (and I'm not sure they would care to be mentioned in this book) do not use toilet paper at all. What do they use? Well, there's a little plastic bowl and a water tap in every stall next to "the hole." The idea is that —as far as tourists are concerned—you look at the water and the little plastic bowl, then pull some toilet paper out of your pocket and use that. But some people, such as everyone who lives in that country, forget to bring toilet paper, so they use the water in conjunction with their left hands. This explains why these people only eat with their right hands. It also explains why they don't pick their noses much.

How to flush "the hole" is not entirely apparent. There's no little handle to push. No knob to turn. And no, I'm not pulling your chain. You have to fill up the plastic bowl a few times, dump the water into The Hole and let physics (or maybe comparative literature) do the rest. It feels more like a religious ritual than a toilet flushing so you may as well take the opportunity to pray that you won't be back any-time soon.

The other sort of toilet looks like a Western model that was creatively installed by someone who couldn't read the English directions that came with the assembly kit. If you're lucky enough to find one with a seat, you'll notice it's usu-ally secured by something with the strength of dental floss—so if you don't sit down exactly straight, the seat de-taches and you slide right off the porcelain rim, which can be pretty painful and embarrassing and not the sort of thing you would ever want to mention in a place where millions of people might read it.[1]

More commonly, however, the plastic seat is missing al-together, perhaps for use as a Third World Frisbee. This means that you are back to squatting again. Only now it's more difficult because you can't do a regular squat; you have to do a "standing squat" so you can clear the rim of the toilet. This usually entails bracing yourself with one hand on the wall behind you, which is highly exhausting for your arm and leg muscles and often makes them cramp painfully.

A few of these bathrooms do come equipped with paper, but it's usually the sort that Rambo would be afraid to use. So you're better off bringing your own. Either way, you should never, not even if the Archbishop of Canterbury gets down on his hands and knees and begs you, even think of throwing your paper into the toilet. There is a little plas-

---

[1] Maybe hundreds of people. Or at least seventy-three people, if you include my extended family.

tic bin nearby for that purpose. These johns, though they may look vaguely like ours, have an allergic reaction to toilet paper: even one square of Charmin can clog them for about a month.

There are a few models I found around the Turkey/ Syria region that have built-in bidets, a French invention that functions like a below-the-waist Waterpik. The idea is that, in lieu (no pun intended) of toilet paper, you can use this device to give yourself a painful enema. The French have a separate machine for this water treatment, but in this region, there's just a bent metal pipe that is aimed...well, you can imagine where it's aimed. The major problem, besides having to grope around behind the tank to find the water-control knob, is that some of these spigots are poorly positioned so that the bent metal pipe is a little higher than it should be, and if you sit down too fast, you might find yourself in the middle of an altogether pretty unpleasant experience, if you know what I mean.

This brings me to my sure-fire adventure travel toilet tips: (1) practice squatting in your living room; (2) use a timer to work on your speed; (3) practice carrying around large quantities of toilet paper, and (4) if you can manage it when you get to your destination, don't go to the bathroom at all.

Glossary

AT THE HOTEL

all-night room service: How long you'll wait before the food is delivered. See: slight additional charge.

award-winning hotel: Has been awarded several subpoenas from the local health authority and the building commission.

continental breakfast: Three-day-old croissant and choice of two milliliters of coffee or two milliliters of juice.

cooled by ocean breezes: The window is broken.

deluxe accommodation: End of toilet-paper roll has been neatly folded.

en suite bathroom: Your room includes the smallest allowable bathroom by European Union building standards.

evening entertainment: A trio of locals on homemade instruments.

family stay: Unique opportunity to be ripped off by a real family—will graciously make room for you to stay in their closet.

friendly staff: Brothel.

inquire at reception: Stand in line at reception.

international calling available from your hotel room: $3 for an outside line, then $12 a minute.

natural surroundings: The nearest Kentucky Fried Chicken cannot be seen from the hotel.

panoramic view: You can see the entire wall of the hotel across the alley.

rustic: Sheets have not been changed since 1971.

slight additional charge: Probably not more than $600.

undiscovered paradise: Not more than five major hotel chains in the vicinity.

unrivaled location: No other hotel requires a two-hour taxi ride.

ON TOUR

all-inclusive: Drinks, snacks, excursions, activities, and tips are not included.

drinks and food are available on board: Don't forget your wallet.

historic old town: Tourist epicenter.

must-see: Might see, if other tourists get out of your way.

natural formations: Potholes.

personalized tour: You can decide when to stop for restroom breaks.

quaint village: Tourists outnumber locals 9 to 1.

rain jacket recommended: Averages three days of sun per year.

toilet on board tour bus: One out of seven people can actually fit into this bathroom.

within walking distance: Can be reached on foot by elite Kenyan runners in less than a day.

world famous: The proprietor's immediate family in his country of origin know about it.

SHOPPING

all major credit cards accepted: With a 5 percent service charge.

bureau de change: Will probably not take a commission higher than the amount of money you are attempting to change.

downtown duty-free shopping: You'll have to carry around a sealed package for the rest of your trip.

special price: Triple what locals pay.

"Where are you from?": Do you come from a country with a strong currency?

"What is your profession?": What is your credit card limit?

DINING OUT

establishment is frequented by locals: Locals will try to sell you roses for $5 each while you dine with other tourists.

fully air-conditioned: No matter what temperature it is outside, the air conditioner will be set on "Turbo Blast" so you can deep-freeze your meal while you eat. Winter jacket is advisable.

international cuisine: McDonald's and Taco Bell nearby.

service included: Lousy service included, extra tip expected.

tourist menu: One meal for the price of two.

unforgettable service: Unforgivable service.

GETTING AROUND

courtesy shuttle will pick you up: Eventually.

easy access to tourist information bureau: A closed tourist information bureau is nearby.

economy class: Seats are designed and engineered for use by yoga professionals and midgets only.

experienced driver: Has been to traffic court numerous times.

tourist facilities available: Gift shops within twenty yards.

"Your luggage will be arriving at Carousel Number Three": Some of your luggage will be arriving at Carousel Number Three.

Doug sleeping in the ice hotel.

About the Author

DOUG LANSKY, A NATIONALLY-SYNDICATED TRAVEL columnist, correspondent for public radio's *The Savvy Traveler*, Discovery Channel host, contributor to various magazines, and editor of the award-winning travel-humor anthology, *There's No Toilet Paper on the Road Less Traveled*, sometimes makes his bed in the morning, but more often than not, he doesn't. He readily admits that he's not particularly gifted in the department of computer science, and fixes just about every problem by turning the computer off and turning it back on again. Which usually seems to do the trick. Even for problems that have nothing to do with the computer. But not making the bed. The Author wears size 10 1/2 shoes, except for the brands that run a bit small. In which case, he'll take an 11. He has been known to gobble, when available, Pop Tarts for breakfast, and is also fond of toasted cinnamon-raisin bagels with cream cheese. However, the Author rarely gets either of these because he spends most of his time in Europe with his Swedish wife, Signe, a medical doctor, who prefers corn flakes and wears a size 8 shoe.